UNITED NATIONS CONFERENCE ON TRADE AND DEVELOPMENT

Forging a Path Beyond Borders:
The Global South

Geneva, 2018

UNCTAD/OSG/2018/1

ISBN: 978-92-1-112936-6
eISBN: 978-92-1-047478-8
Sales No. E.19.II.D.2

Acknowledgements

The report, *Forging a Path Beyond Borders: The Global South*, was prepared by an interdivisional team of the United Nations Conference on Trade and Development, under the leadership of Daniel Owoko. The team members were Anida Yupari Aguado, Bineswaree Bolaky, Christopher Garroway de Coninck, Kee Hwee Wee, Luisa Rodriguez, Rashmi Banga, Taisuke Ito, Yan Zhang and Yongfu Ouyang.

A special word of recognition goes to the Technical Cooperation Section and the five Divisions of the United Nations Conference on Trade and Development for the inputs and comments received, through members of the interdivisional team, as well as for support received from the UNCTAD New York Office.

An earlier draft of the report benefited from extensive discussions and recommendations provided at an informal thematic consultation held on 5 November 2018.

The thematic consultation was organized by the United Nations Conference on Trade and Development, in cooperation with the Permanent Mission of the Argentine Republic to the United Nations Office and other international organizations in Geneva.

The report was edited by Maritza Ascencios. Magali Studer, Nadège Hadjemian and Pablo Cortizo designed the report. Support from Kseniia Pavlenko, Lucy Deleze-Black and Pavel Skomorokhin is also gratefully acknowledged. Angela Prescott, Candy Catala, Evelyn Benitez, Jayne Dawson and Séverine Excoffier provided logistical support.

Foreword

The "rise of the South", as some have called it, has prompted much speculation about the "decoupling" of growth in developing countries from that of advanced economies. This phenomenon has likewise led to much enthusiasm about new approaches to global governance. Yet, for as much as the so-called rise of the South has prompted enthusiasm, that "rise" has also been relatively uneven and incomplete. The idea that developing countries can become engines of the global economy remains on the whole unrealized, and the structural economic barriers that still hold back the world's least developed countries keep them, in many cases, dependent on commodities and vulnerable to external shocks.

So, what does the future of cooperation among economies of the global South hold for developing countries? The report prepared by the United Nations Conference on Trade and Development (UNCTAD), *Forging a Path Beyond Borders: The Global South,* analyses the rising global South – past and present – with an eye to reinvigorating this important and unique source of development cooperation. The report analyses the main challenges and opportunities in South–South trade, investment and finance and emphasizes growing opportunities for South–South cooperation on technology transfers and partnerships for technological innovation, as well as the suitable policies needed, to kick off innovative partnerships in key emerging areas such as "Industry 4.0".

This report was informed by an earlier draft version, presented at an informal thematic consultation, held on 5 November 2018 and organized by UNCTAD in cooperation with the Permanent Mission of the Argentine Republic to the United Nations Office and other international organizations in Geneva. The outcome of the consultation and a set of non-binding recommendations are included in this final report.

In the lead up to the Second High-level United Nations Conference on South–South Cooperation – the BAPA+40 Conference – to be held in Buenos Aires from 20 to 22 March 2019, it is my pleasure to present this UNCTAD report. I hope that its seven analytical chapters, the outcome of the informal thematic consultation and the non-binding recommendations are considered by Member States during the negotiations on a forward-looking outcome document to be adopted at BAPA+40 Conference. These elements offer a novel angle on underlying issues and practical suggestions for countries of the South to consider when preparing strategies or implementing action plans for achieving the 2030 Agenda for Sustainable Development and the Sustainable Development Goals.

Mukhisa Kituyi
Secretary-General
United Nations Conference on Trade and Development

Abbreviations

ASEAN	Association of Southeast Asian Nations
ASMP	ASYCUDA Support Mechanism for the Pacific
ASYCUDA	Automated System for Customs Data
BAPA	Buenos Aires Plan of Action for Promoting and Implementing Technical Cooperation among Developing Countries
BRICS	Brazil, Russian Federation, India, China and South Africa
CAF	Development Bank of Latin America (Andean Development Corporation)
COMESA	Common Market for Eastern and Southern Africa
EAC	East African Community
ECOWAS	Economic Community of West African States
ERIA	Economic Research Institute for ASEAN and South East Asia
FDI	foreign direct investment
GDP	gross domestic product
GVC	global value chain
ICT	information and communications technology
LDC	least developed country
RVC	regional value chain
SADC	Southern African Development Community
SIDS	small island developing States
SSE	Sustainable Stock Exchanges Initiative (of the United Nations)
UNCTAD	United Nations Conference on Trade and Development

Contents

Figures

Boxes

Table

Executive summary

The "rise of the South", as some have called it, has prompted much speculation about the "decoupling" of growth in developing countries from that of advanced economies. This phenomenon has likewise led to much enthusiasm about new approaches to global governance. Examples are expansion of the Group of Eight to the Group of 20, as one response to the global financial crisis a decade ago; the emergence of Brazil, the Russian Federation, India, China and South Africa – the BRICS countries – as a grouping of major developing countries, which now meets regularly; and new sources of Southern-led development finance, such as the New Development Bank (i.e. the "BRICS bank") and the Asian Infrastructure Infrastructure Bank.

Forging a Path Beyond Borders: The Global South shows that the past 40 years, since the Buenos Aires Plan of Action for Promoting and Implementing Technical Cooperation among Developing Countries in 1978, have indeed seen an explosion of intensified cooperation within and across the global South, with the emergence of developing countries as regional and global players in almost every region. Today, South–South trade accounts for more than one quarter of world trade, and foreign direct investment (FDI) outflows from Southern firms account for around one third of global FDI flows. And thanks to high-growth developing economies, the South has contributed to more than half of global growth in recent years.

Yet, for as much as the so-called rise of the South has prompted enthusiasm, that "rise" has also been relatively uneven and incomplete. The idea that developing countries can become engines of the global economy remains on the whole unrealized. A widespread shift towards economic convergence between the North and the South, observed broadly in developing countries in the first decade of the 2000s, turns out not to have been so. Rather, it was largely a super cycle commodity boom driven mainly by China, which has since receded with falling commodity prices. Nor was the boom sustained in the decade since the crisis.

The rise in South–South flows has managed, though, to shift many attitudes about the differences between North and South. What it has not erased are the structural economic barriers that still hold back the world's least developed countries (LDCs) and keep them, to a large degree, dependent on commodities and vulnerable to external shocks.

So, what does the future of cooperation among economies of the global South hold for developing countries? This report analyses the rising global South – past and present – from the perspective of how to reinvigorate this important and unique source of development cooperation. The report considers the evolution of South–South cooperation, particularly over the last 40 years, and ways for economies of the global South to work beyond their borders in today's world, while taking into account topical issues such as regional cooperation and digital industrialization.

Three objectives, crucial to achieving the 2030 Agenda for Sustainable Development and its Sustainable Development Goals, provide the basis for this report's analysis, namely identifying: (a) the main challenges and opportunities in South–South trade, investment and financing issues and identification of relevant policies; (b) opportunities for South–South cooperation on technology transfers and partnerships for technological innovation; and (c) challenges and opportunities and suitable policies for innovative South–South cooperation and partnerships in key emerging areas such as "Industry 4.0".

> Yet, the idea of developing countries as engines of the global economy remains on the whole unrealized.

> Today, trade among developing countries of the South accounts for more than 25% of world trade.

Chapter 1 of this report presents the evidence behind the qualitative and quantitative changes observed in South–South cooperation over the past four decades. Chapter 2 looks at the link between South–South cooperation and the means of implementation for the Sustainable Development Goals, particularly with respect to trade and development issues. Taking the specific example of Sustainable Development Goal 7, with a view to transformational energy access, it also highlights how South–South cooperation can provide critical solutions to the global South's development challenges. Chapter 3 examines policy options in domains that can help improve South–South cooperation, drawing from a range of UNCTAD experience. Chapter 4 looks at the new panorama of Southern development finance actors and how developing countries can leverage this emerging area of South–South cooperation as one way to finance connectivity, structural transformation and industrialization. Chapter 5 explores key and emerging areas for South–South cooperation, including regional cooperation, building productive capacity and responsible investment. Chapter 6 hones in on best practices in South–South cooperation taken from UNCTAD technical cooperation experience. Chapter 7 looks at the role that South–South cooperation can play in the light of new technologies, particularly so-called fourth industrial revolution technologies.

The conclusions drawn from this report's analysis, and an informal thematic consultation organized by UNCTAD in the lead up to the BAPA+40 Conference, are presented as recommendations (see annex)[1]. These recommendations intersect with the topics covered in the following chapters, but also offer a novel angle on underlying issues and practical suggestions for countries of the South to consider when preparing strategies or implementing action plans for achieving the 2030 Agenda and its Sustainable Development Goals.

It is the hope of UNCTAD that the non-binding recommendations that came out of the informal thematic consultation, presented below, inform and contribute to the negotiations of Member States on a forward-looking outcome document, to be adopted by the BAPA+40 Conference in Buenos Aires in 2019.

- South–South cooperation should be strengthened to help developing countries make the most of vibrant South–South trade, finance, investment and technology for sustainable development. Regional and country experiences need to be analysed to fully understand why the "rise of the South" has been uneven and release the catalytic potential of South–South growth.

- Innovations and deeper interactions in South–South financial and monetary cooperation should be seen as the foundations for providing pragmatic options that address Southern concerns, within the global system.

- South–South cooperation should be seen as a complement to, not a substitute for, North–South cooperation. Official development assistance commitments need to be met and deficiencies of the multilateral institutions addressed as well.

- South–South cooperation should support building productive capacity and structural transformation in the South, especially in Africa and LDCs. Strategic engagement with South–South value chains is needed to drive upgrading and diversification.

- Latin America, Asia and Africa need to strengthen partnerships across regions in order to spur trade and investment cooperation.

- The BAPA+40 Conference should provide broad-based support for revitalizing South–South trade cooperation at the interregional level, including through the Global System of Trade Preferences among Developing Countries.

In what ways can economies of the global South work beyond their borders in today's world?

[1] In addition to the recommendations, the annex contains a summary of all sessions of the informal thematic consultation.

- South–South technology transfers and partnerships should be promoted for technological innovation via, for example, platforms enabling "matchmaking" between developing countries that develop technology and those that demand such technology and mechanisms (such as the United Nations Commission on Science and Technology for Development) that facilitate sharing of successful experiences among Southern countries. UNCTAD and other relevant international organizations can provide the technical assistance developing countries could require to enable them to access technologies.

- Developing countries of the South should form the necessary partnerships to meet the challenges posed by Industry 4.0. South–South digital cooperation is also key to promoting digital industrialization in the South.

- Policies for promoting electronic commerce (e-commerce) should be complemented by appropriate digital industrial policymaking in Africa to ensure the region harnesses the broader benefits of digitalization.

- Developing countries, especially in Africa, and LDCs need to coordinate their position on future rules at the World Trade Organization in relation to e-commerce and digital trade, taking into account their policy space to engage in industrialization.

Introduction

Economic cooperation among developing countries, especially through trade, was one of the founding principles behind the establishment of UNCTAD – the United Nations Conference on Trade and Development – more than half a century ago. Raúl Prebisch, in his report to the first session of the Conference in 1964, argued for increased South–South trade, including through preferential regional and intraregional trading arrangements among groupings of developing countries. At the time, he called the approach "a new trade policy for development".

Today, the case for expanding trade and investment links within the South is a part of the economic mainstream. Indeed, acceptance of the importance of this view can be traced back largely to the United Nations Conference on Technical Cooperation among Developing Countries, held in Buenos Aires in 1978, which resulted in agreement on the Buenos Aires Plan of Action for Promoting and Implementing Technical Cooperation among Developing Countries (BAPA). In 2009, the Nairobi outcome document adopted at the High-level United Nations Conference on South–South Cooperation further reinforced the view, by recognizing that international support for South–South cooperation in trade and investment can be catalytic for strengthening and consolidating regional and subregional economic integration.

Much has changed in terms of the scope and importance of South–South cooperation. It is thus fitting that Buenos Aires is to again host a high-level United Nations conference on South–South cooperation on the fortieth anniversary of the adoption of the Buenos Aires Plan of Action for Promoting and Implementing Technical Cooperation among Developing Countries.

The Second High-level United Nations Conference on South–South Cooperation on the occasion of the fortieth anniversary of the adoption of the Buenos Aires Plan of Action – the BAPA+40 Conference (box) – will take stock and review lessons learned over the past four decades, with a view to implementing an inclusive strategy that effectively leverages South–South collaborative efforts and approaches to achieving sustainable development for all. In echoing the aim of 2030 Agenda for Sustainable Development of leaving no one behind, the BAPA+40 Conference is also an opportunity for the international community to spur concerted and collaborative actions by developing countries, through partnerships involving all stakeholders, to bolster the role of South–South cooperation in support of its implementation. South–South cooperation is recognized as one of the major means of implementation for advancing the 2030 Agenda for Sustainable Development. Target 17.9 of the Sustainable Development Goals, for instance, calls on stakeholders to "enhance international support for implementing effective and targeted capacity-building in developing countries to support national plans to implement all the Sustainable Development Goals, including through North–South, South–South and triangular cooperation".[2]

Against that backdrop, three objectives, crucial to achieving the 2030 Agenda for Sustainable Development and its Sustainable Development Goals, provide the basis for this report's analysis, namely identifying: (a) the main challenges and opportunities in South–South trade, investment and financing issues and identification of relevant policies; (b) opportunities for South–South cooperation on technology transfers and partnerships for technological innovation; and (c) challenges and opportunities and suitable policies for innovative South–South cooperation and partnerships in key emerging areas such as "Industry 4.0".

The BAPA+40 Conference, March 2019

Overarching theme

The role of South–South cooperation and implementation of the 2030 Agenda for Sustainable Development: Challenges and opportunities

Sub-themes

a. Comparative advantages of and opportunities for South–South cooperation;

b. Challenges and the strengthening of the institutional framework of South–South cooperation and triangular cooperation;

c. Sharing of experiences, best practices and success stories;

d. Scaling up the means of implementation of the 2030 Agenda in support of South–South cooperation and triangular cooperation.

---

[2] The role of the global South in development has also been recognized in major United Nations conference outcome documents, such as in paragraph 12 of the Programme of Action for the Least Developed Countries for the Decade 2011–2020 (Istanbul Programme of Action), paragraph 99 of the SIDS Accelerated Modalities of Action (SAMOA) Pathway and paragraph 16 of the Programme of Action for Landlocked Developing Countries for the Decade 2014–2024 (Vienna Programme of Action).

> **South–South cooperation is a recognized major means of implementation for advancing the 2030 Agenda**

The conclusions drawn from this report's analysis, and from an informal thematic consultation organized by UNCTAD in the lead up to the BAPA+40 Conference (see annex), resulting in non-binding recommendations, intersect with the topics covered in the following chapters. The report is thus envisaged as a contribution to negotiations on a forward-looking outcome document during the Second High-level United Nations Conference on South–South Cooperation. It also offers a novel angle on key issues and practical suggestions for countries of the South to consider in the long term, when preparing strategies or implementing action plans for achieving the 2030 Agenda for Sustainable Development and the Sustainable Development Goals.

CHAPTER 1

Tracing the rise and challenges of the global South

1.1 A tangible rise, but not for all

The South's contribution to growth of world trade reached about 50% in the 2000s.

Growth in global trade has outpaced growth in global output since the 1950s. Looking back even further, from the late nineteenth century to the present, what is apparent – and striking – is that the share of developing countries in global trade and global production has been rising over time (figure 1). Yet only since the mid-1980s has the share of the South in global trade and output begun to rise rapidly. From 1990 until the global financial crisis of 2008/09, growth of world trade in real terms increased to more than 6 per cent, with the contribution of the South reaching about 50 per cent in the 2000s.[3]

Delving into what lies behind some of these figures, first, South–South exports grew at an annual average rate of 13 per cent between 1995 and 2016, far outpacing total world exports, at 8 per cent. The value of South–South trade increased almost seven-fold, from just $0.6 trillion in 1995 to $4 trillion in 2016. The share of South–South trade in developing countries' total exports rose from 42 per cent to 57 per cent. In 2016, one quarter – 25 per cent – of world total trade took place among developing countries.

Notably, though, acceleration in the growth of output and trade in 1990s was concentrated in a few developing countries. A closer look at growth in the South in terms of global trade reveals that Asia alone accounted for 93 per cent of South–South trade in manufactures in 2016. Of that, the share for East Asia was 72 per cent.

[3] UNCTAD, 2018a.

Annual growth rates of global trade and global production
(Percentage)

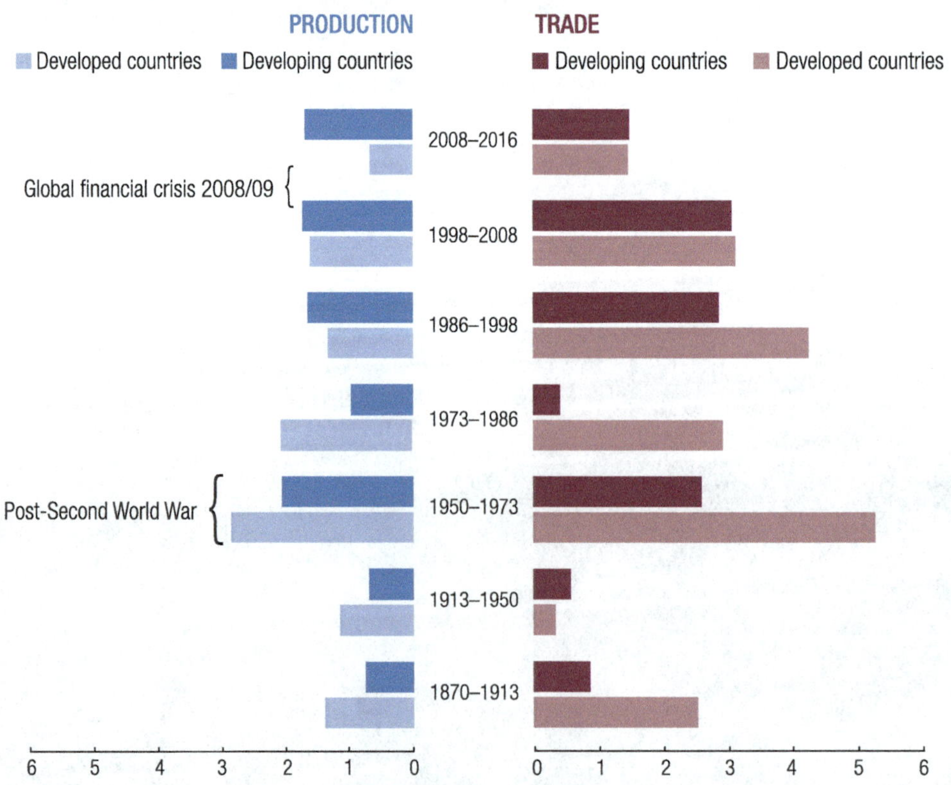

Source: UNCTAD, 2018a.
Note: Light colours represent the contribution of developed countries to the corresponding world aggregates. Data represent real annual compound growth rates, computed using constant 1990 dollars between 1870 and 1998 and constant 2010 dollars between 1998 and 2016.

Growth in trade was strongest in East and South-East Asian economies, particularly in the first-tier newly industrializing economies, the Asian Tigers, i.e. Hong Kong (China), Taiwan Province of China, the Republic of Korea and Singapore. Nevertheless, it was growth in the second-tier newly industrializing economies – namely, Indonesia, Malaysia, the Philippines and Thailand – that supported growth in the four Asian Tigers. It was this interdependence of trade that led to emergence of global value chains (GVCs), which relied heavily on intra-industry trade within Asia. The significant expansion of exports in all of these Asian economies was followed by rapid growth in exports from China. In 2004, China overtook Japan as the largest exporter in the region and, in 2007, became the largest exporter in the world.

Growth in Asia, particularly in China, spilled over to other developing countries, in Africa and elsewhere, mainly in the form of growing demand for raw materials. As a result, South–South trade witnessed rapid growth. Between 1990 and 2016, the share of world exports to developing countries and transition economies increased from 26 per cent to 47 per cent. South–South trade accounted for more than half of this increase.[4]

The advent and rapid expansion of FDI originating from developing countries in recent years has also lent an important new "Southern" dimension to international investment. Total FDI outflows from firms of developing economies grew significantly over the last decade, from around $110 billion in 2005 to $381 billion in 2017, and now constitute almost 30 per cent of global flows (figure 2). Increasingly, multinational enterprises from emerging economies have become involved in foreign projects. The value of greenfield and cross-border merger and acquisitions tripled in the 10 years to 2016. The largest outward investing developing economies now include China, Hong Kong (China), Singapore, Brazil, Republic of Korea, Taiwan Province of China, South Africa, Mexico, India, Malaysia, United Arab Emirates and Chile, as ranked by outward FDI stock.

> **Growth in Asia spilled over to developing countries in Africa and elsewhere, through growing demand for raw materials.**

[4] UNCTAD, 2018a.

Developing economies: Foreign direct investment outflows

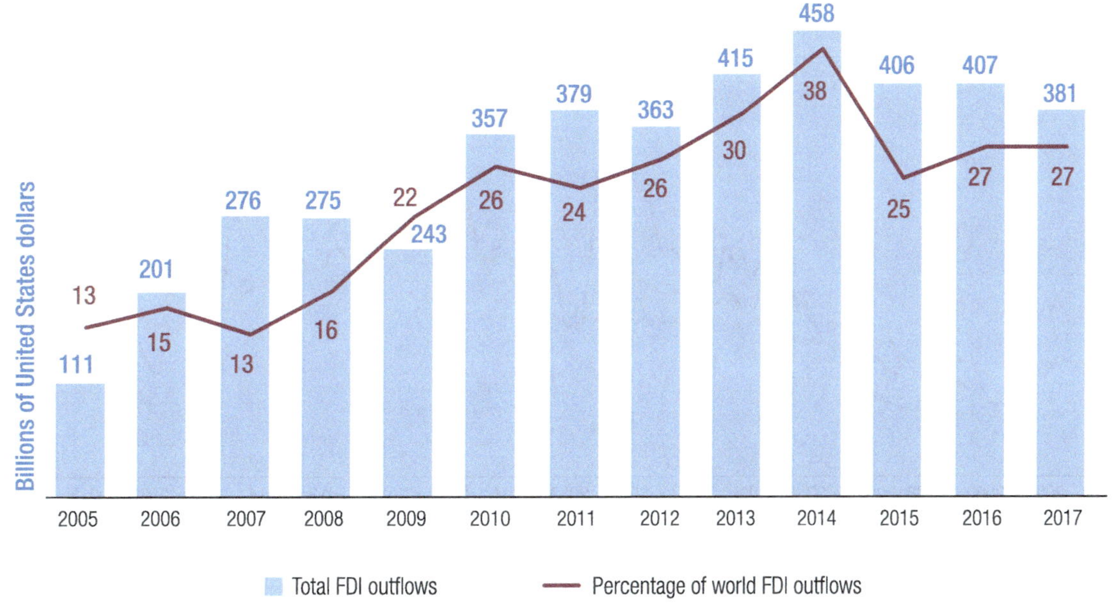

Source: UNCTAD calculations.

The rise in FDI from developing economies is particularly relevant to low-income countries, as most outflows are to other developing countries. For example, 6 developing economies featured among the top 10 economies investing in LDCs in 2016. FDI outward stock from developing economies to other developing economies, excluding Caribbean offshore financial centres, more than doubled from an estimated $1.7 trillion in 2010, to $4.1 trillion in 2016. This accounted for almost 70 per cent of their total outward stock. In some cases – for example, Cambodia, Namibia, Mozambique, Myanmar, Sri Lanka and Togo – Southern investors already account for the majority of a country's FDI stock.

The growth of the South, spearheaded by growth in a handful of Asian countries, fuelled by trade expansion and reinforced by increased South–South investment and the spread of GVCs, has led many to uphold the phenomenon as the rise of South or the "great convergence".[5] However, the commensurate super cycle in commodities observed in the 2000s, coupled with unsustained growth for commodity-exporting countries following this period, underscores the fact that growth in the South has not led to structural transformation.

The commodity price boom (2003–2011), spurred on partly by increased demand for raw materials in developing Asia, was a boon for many commodity-dependent developing countries. These countries registered a large increase in export revenues and, generally, in their economic growth rates. Then, as the boom came to an end, commodity-dependent developing countries were reminded that, as the Prebisch–Singer hypothesis argues, a few years of strong commodity prices do not alter the long-term pattern of their terms of trade. Specifically, the terms of trade of economies dependent on primary commodities tend to deteriorate, in the long run, as primary commodity prices also naturally decline relative to the prices of manufactured goods. It is currently widely believed that prices will remain at lower levels in the medium term, given that growth in emerging economies has decelerated and, in general, commodity supply has not fully adjusted to consequent weaker demand (figure 3).

---

[5] See United Nations Development Programme, 2013, and Baldwin, 2011.

Free market commodity price indices
(2015=100)

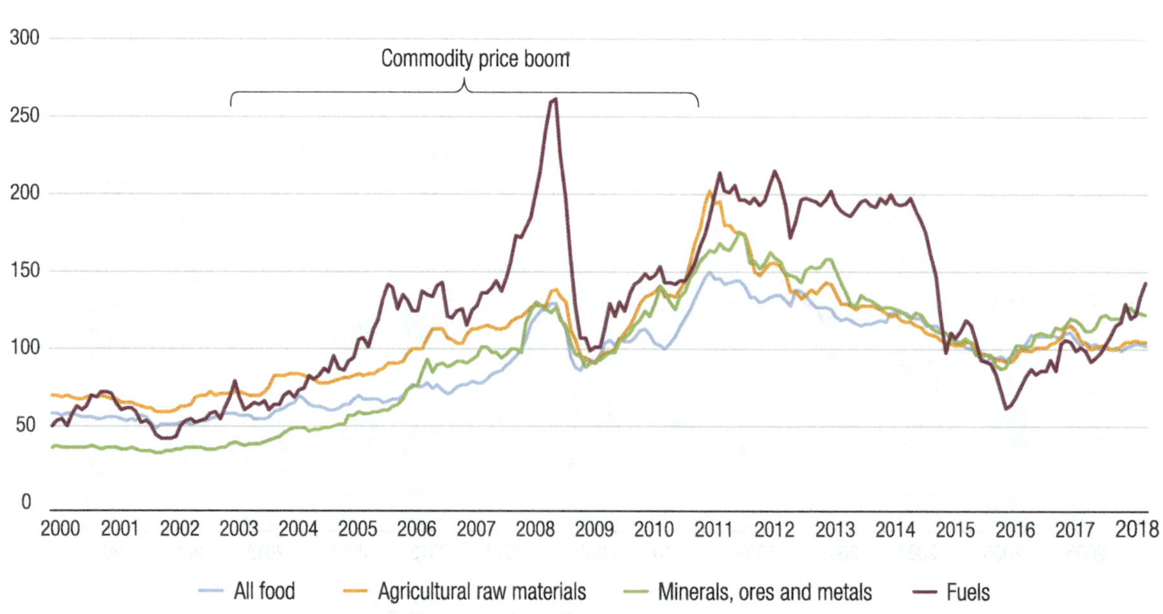

Source: UNCTADstat database.
Note: Trends in indices reflect data on a monthly basis, from January 2000 through May 2018.
[a] Not all minerals, ores and metals saw a commodity price boom.

Across domestic economies of many developing countries and in particular LDCs, especially commodity-exporting countries, growth has generated few linkages to development. In such cases, increased trade has led to hyperglobalization rather than genuine development, inclusiveness or sustainability.[6] Linking into GVCs has increased trade figures in the South but with limited matching increases in domestic value addition to countries' exports (UNCTAD, 2015a). Rather, "lead" corporations, those that outsource selected activities to specific locations and manage the assembly, branding and marketing of the final product, have played a central role and extracted maximum rents (UNCTAD, 2016a). Hyperglobalization in the past three decades has led to considerable concentration of economic power and wealth in the hands of a few transnational corporations and promoted "profits without prosperity". This asymmetric market power has led to rising income inequality, accentuating economic and social vulnerability in the South.[7]

The rapid growth of market concentration and rent-seeking tendencies, and the fact that headquarters of the top transnational corporations are located mainly in the North, underscores how moderate the so-called "rise of the South" has been, apart from China, and how far-fetched claims of a "great convergence" remain.[8] The global economy has been characterized by rising market concentration and rent extraction, which can feed off one another, resulting in a "winner-takes-most competition" that, in many developed economies, has become a visible part of the corporate environment.[9] The global South, on the other hand, has become more vulnerable with rising numbers of small and medium-sized enterprises, growing informal sectors, rising poverty, inequality and unemployment.

1.2 Persistent challenges of the most vulnerable countries

The multiple challenges and vulnerabilities developing countries face have been well researched and documented.[10] LDCs are home to the poorest and most vulnerable segments of the global population. For these countries, the road to addressing sustainable development challenges remains long and bumpy. The 32 landlocked developing countries – situated in Africa, Asia, Europe and South America – are faced with special challenges arising from their lack of direct territorial access to the sea and their remoteness and isolation from world markets. Of note, they are dependent on the political, economic and environmental situation of their neighbouring countries. Most economic studies that have analysed the impact of a geographically landlocked position on economic growth have found that lack of direct access to the sea represents a constraint. Controlling for other determinants, the growth rate of landlocked countries has been found, on average, to be at least 3.5 percentage points below that of other countries; and this effect cannot be entirely offset, even by domestic policies conducive to growth (UNCTAD, 2016c). Small island developing States (SIDS) also face unique development challenges, as they are particularly vulnerable to climate change and its economic and social consequences.

Among many sustainable development challenges and vulnerabilities are volatile economic growth, an overreliance on commodity production and exports, weak productive capacities, lack of structural transformation, pervasive infrastructure deficits, insufficient domestic resource mobilization amidst limited financing for development, weak export competitiveness, continued vulnerability to economic, social and environmental shocks and disasters, gender inequality, growing youth unemployment, weak human capacities, rural–urban disparities and a need to strengthen developmental governance and capacities of the public and private sectors.[11]

South–South cooperation has the potential to overcome specific vulnerabilities.

[7] Ibid.

[8] UNCTAD, 2018a.

[9] Ibid.

[10] Listed in outcome documents of major United Nations conferences, e.g. the Istanbul Programme of Action. Similarly, the Vienna Programme of Action and the SAMOA Pathway. In 2015, the 2030 Agenda for Sustainable Development of the United Nations also firmly put a spotlight on the multiple vulnerabilities that continue to afflict developing countries, especially in Africa, LDCs, landlocked developing countries and small island developing States (paragraph, 16). The 2030 Agenda calls for a revitalized Global Partnership for Sustainable Development to address the scourge of extreme poverty and hunger in the developing world, combat the growing income inequalities that exist between developed and developing countries and inside national borders and tackle the acceleration of global environmental challenges that can derail progress towards prosperity for all.

[11] Challenges analysed for more than a decade in The Least Developed Countries Report series of UNCTAD. UNCTAD, 2006; UNCTAD, 2017b; UNCTAD, 2016a; and UNCTAD, 2015a.

Economic, social and environmental vulnerabilities are interlinked both at the national and international levels. Coupled with the associated regional and global spillover effects, this means that addressing the consequent development challenges requires increased collaboration and coordination within the global South and between developing countries and development partners. It also calls for adoption of a holistic approach to make the most of synergies and complementarities across development interventions.

It is here that South–South cooperation and triangular cooperation have the potential to overcome these specific vulnerabilities.[12] The global South can play a vital role in strengthening capacities of small island developing States in sustainable trade and in building a sustainable blue economy through increased South–South cooperation. Similarly, transport, transit infrastructure and trade facilitation are areas where South–South cooperation plays a key role, in particular in landlocked developing countries[13] where it is imperative to develop adequate transport and transit infrastructure and trade facilitation to promote sound integration into regional and global markets.

1.3 Counteracting pervasive commodity dependence

The majority of developing countries are commodity dependent.[14] Developing countries dependent on commodity exports derive the bulk of their export earnings from primary commodities such as minerals, ores, metals, fuels, agricultural raw materials and food.[15] Countries that have a high ratio of commodity imports to total merchandise trade are considered dependent on commodity imports.[16] On the basis of 189 United Nations Member States, 64 per cent of developing countries are dependent on commodity exports and 45 per cent are dependent on commodity imports. Commodity dependence is particularly prevalent among LDCs, where 79 per cent are dependent on commodity exports and 56 per cent are dependent on commodity imports.

Both forms of commodity dependence can have potentially harmful impacts and affect all dimensions of sustainable development. Most developing countries that depend on commodity exports and/or imports are characterized by low human development. The effects of commodity dependence on human development are mitigated through numerous direct and indirect channels that link global commodity markets with domestic economic, social and human development conditions. Economic performance is associated with how the commodity sector evolves in these countries (box 1).

Yet, commodities can bring in large revenues and create important opportunities for economic growth and sustainable development. A decisive factor in making this a reality is adding value to commodities. Most commodity-dependent developing countries, however, export their commodities as raw materials, rather than going through any production process. With the potential of commodities unattended to, these countries have been hard pressed to transform the wealth of their extractive sector into economic or sustainable development gains that benefit the rest of the economy. Value addition is therefore a central component of commodity-led development strategies. These include moving up the value chain and increasing the volume of a country's export products and broadening markets.

Cooperation between developing countries of the global South can work to add value to commodity exports, moving from raw materials to finished products. For instance, UNCTAD capacity-building projects, typically focused on value addition and export diversification, assist developing countries in overcoming the policy,

---

Adding value to commodities is decisive in creating opportunities for economic growth and sustainable development.

---

[12] See the Istanbul Programme of Action which identifies South–South cooperation as one of its means of implementation, as a complement to and not substitute for North–South cooperation (paragraph 26(f)).

[13] As underscored in paragraph 70 of the Vienna Programme of Action.

[14] UNCTAD and Food and Agriculture Organization of the United Nations (2017).

[15] Defined as countries that generate more than 60 per cent of their merchandise export revenues from food, agricultural raw materials, minerals, ores and metals and/or energy-related commodities.

[16] Defined as countries whose share of value of food and fuel imports in total merchandise imports exceeds 30 per cent.

Box 1

The long reach of commodity price fluctuations

The relationship between the selling prices of a country's exports and the prices paid for its imports – the terms of trade – of commodity-dependent developing countries is closely linked to commodity prices. In developing countries dependent on commodity exports, a sudden drop in commodity prices generally causes a shock in the terms of trade, which in turn translates into an output shock that adversely affects growth prospects. Even in the absence of large shocks, commodity price volatility harms growth in commodity-dependent developing countries. As growth is a prerequisite for the elimination of poverty, there is a link between price movements on global commodity markets and human development in these countries. In other words, through the terms-of-trade channel, commodity price movements transmit a range of economic and non-economic impacts on human development, both direct and indirect and over the short and long term.

Commodity dependence is also a potential source of fiscal and monetary stress. Strong fluctuations of capital flows, such as those induced by commodity price volatility, cause economic disruption and put pressure on the balance of payments. Government revenue in commodity-dependent developing countries is also typically closely linked to commodity prices. When commodity prices are lower than expected, this can undermine the fiscal balance and reduce policy space, which then causes a decline in public spending on crucial infrastructure and social programmes, thereby hindering national economic development and poverty alleviation efforts. On the other hand, imported inflation is another risk that developing countries dependent on commodity imports face.

Specifically, in countries with greater food imports than food exports (net food-importing countries), food price hikes can erode real incomes and thus increase poverty. This was observed in several countries during the global financial and food crises of 2007 and 2008. Furthermore, commodity price shocks can compromise the debt sustainability of commodity-dependent developing countries where public finance largely depends on revenues from commodity exports.

Finally, commodity price fluctuations can also affect the exchange rates of commodity-dependent developing countries, with adverse impacts on long-term productivity growth, inflation and foreign currency reserves. Commodity price shocks and volatility also have direct impacts on the livelihoods of poor households in developing countries, regardless of whether they depend on commodity exports or imports. Food commodity price shocks can have significant negative effects in developing countries with large agricultural sectors, and where food constitutes a large share of consumer expenditure.

Source: UNCTAD.

information and skills gaps they face in implementing commodity-led development strategies. South–South cooperation features in these projects.

A recent project aimed at strengthening the linkages with development of the mineral resources sector in Central Africa.[17] Through the project, between 2015 and 2017, UNCTAD assisted policymakers and local suppliers in Chad and the Congo with mainstreaming local content into the oil sector. These countries benefited specifically from South–South cooperation through study tours to two developing countries, Angola and Ecuador, that had developed effective local content frameworks. The study tours provided excellent opportunities for participants to learn from relevant experiences of other developing countries that, unlike advanced economies, share a similar economic and development context.

In 2016, another project[18] began work on promoting cotton by-products in Eastern and Southern Africa – specifically, Uganda, the United Republic of Tanzania, Zambia and Zimbabwe. The project is providing assistance to policymakers and commercial stakeholders on strategies for new value added products that make use of different parts of the cotton plant. UNCTAD has engaged the Central Institute for Research on Cotton Technology, in India, to present its innovative cotton by-product technologies. How cotton is produced in India resembles the approach of many African countries: mainly smallholder farmers using manual techniques and, thus, achieving low yields. The Central Institute's technologies are thus well

[17] United Nations Development Account Project 1617K.

[18] United Nations Development Account Project 1617K.

[19] As reflected in the Addis Ababa Action Agenda, achieving the post-2015 sustainable development agenda requires "an equally ambitious, comprehensive, holistic and transformative approach with respect to the means of implementation, combining different means of implementation and integrating the economic, social and environmental dimensions of sustainable development" (paragraph 11). The Addis Ababa Action Agenda has committed both developed and developing countries to move from an official development assistance-centred model of development cooperation towards one of increased domestic resource mobilization.

[20] Section E of the Addis Ababa Action Agenda urges developing countries to engage in prudent debt management while encouraging international institutions to continue to assist developing countries in building debt management capacities and managing risks, building resilience to external shocks and analysing trade-offs between different sources of financing.

[21] Global debt reached a record US$247.2 trillion in March 2018, following a US$8 trillion increase in the first quarter of 2018, according to data from the Institute of International Finance. In aggregate terms, this amounts to 318 per cent of GDP for that period, marking the first increase since 2016. This total debt includes debt owed by households, Governments and financial and non-financial corporations. The increase marks the highest level to date and is of concern as it involves an increase in both the level of debt and its ratio to GDP. The increase leaves some countries particularly vulnerable to debt difficulties in the current economic environment. See Institute of International Finance, 2018.

[22] The debt to GDP ratio increased from 25 per cent in 2011 to 31 per cent in 2017, while the debt service to exports ratio almost quadrupled, rising from 3.8 per cent in 2011 to 12.9 per cent in 2017. A dramatic deterioration in the debt service to government revenue ratio also occurred, which stood at 5 per cent in 2011 and soared to 18.5 per cent in 2017.

suited to the African context. Among the project's activities through 2019 are a study tour to the Central Institute for Research on Cotton Technology that is being planned to familiarize participants with priority technologies. The project will then follow up to assist countries in establishing pilot commercial initiatives.

1.4 Mobilizing finance and debt management

It is well documented that, to achieve the Sustainable Development Goals by 2030,[19] developing countries will require a significant amount of additional financial resources. Preliminary forecasts by UNCTAD in 2014, for instance, already showed that, globally, total investment needs to achieve the Sustainable Development Goals could reach $5 trillion–$7 trillion per year between 2015 and 2030. Investment needs in key sectors of developing countries related to the Goals could reach $3.3 trillion–$4.5 trillion per year for basic infrastructure (roads, rail and ports; power stations; and water and sanitation), food security (agriculture and rural development), climate change mitigation and adaptation, health and education. At current investment levels (both public and private) of $1.4 trillion per year in sectors related to the Goals, there would still be an annual funding gap of up to $2.5 trillion in developing countries (UNCTAD, 2014a).

In the context of the 2030 Agenda, the scale, complexity and breadth of financing for the sustainable development needs of developing countries imply that all development financing options should be considered. This includes resorting to borrowing, at the domestic and international levels, and going into debt.[20] Yet, debt sustainability remains a growing area of concern in many developing countries, and in particular LDCs, as they strive to achieve sustainable development.

Standard external debt indicators for emerging market countries are better than those for developing countries as a group, but relatively easy access to international capital markets exposes them to a specific set of vulnerabilities, largely driven by non-financial corporate borrowing. The Institute of International Finance reports[21] that debt of non-financial corporations increased by $1.5 trillion in the first quarter of 2018, to $31.5 trillion. The ratio of this debt to gross domestic product (GDP) is 94.4 per cent of GDP, higher than 89.4 per cent found in developed countries. Borrowing from international capital markets by non-financial corporates in emerging markets has grown rapidly since 2000. High levels of corporate leverage have made these economies vulnerable to changes in interest rates of the United States of America, appreciation of the United States dollar and monetary policy decisions in developed economies. Recent currency crises in Argentina, Hungary, Indonesia and Turkey highlight how these economies remain vulnerable to adverse investor sentiments and sudden stops of private capital inflows as well as domestic capital flight.

In the case of vulnerable economies, from 2011 to 2017, some of the debt indicators for LDCs show a marked deterioration.[22] These trends are due in part to newly acquired access to global capital markets following a decrease in debt stocks after benefiting from multilateral debt relief initiatives, such as the Heavily Indebted Poor Countries Initiative and the Multilateral Debt Relief Initiative. Countries increased lending on commercial terms to these LDCs over these years, implying substantially higher debt servicing costs. In parallel, this period witnessed weak commodity prices which negatively affected both export and government revenues. The combined effect of these trends has led to a drop in both the numerator and denominator of key debt ratios, giving rise to increased fragility in the financial position of many LDCs.

The International Monetary Fund[23] reports that 40 per cent of low-income developing countries, about twice as many as in 2013, are currently at high risk of debt distress. Moreover, 10 of 13 countries that have moved into the high-risk category since 2013 are in sub-Saharan Africa. Many countries in the region benefited from debt relief provided by the Heavily Indebted Poor Countries Initiative and the Multilateral Debt Relief Initiative, which significantly reduced their debt burdens. While current debt levels have not reached previous highs, these sub-Saharan countries face considerable risk to their debt sustainability as a larger share of debt is issued on commercial terms at higher interest rates and with shorter timelines for reaching maturity. This situation means there will be greater challenges to attain debt resolution, as a result of the more diverse creditor base, namely a greater share of commercial creditors. Any type of debt resolution at a time of crisis would come up against significantly greater challenges in creditor coordination than would be the case when dealing only with multilateral creditors and Governments. The risk here is that countries could slide back into a debt trap that could undermine economic growth and achievement of the Sustainable Development Goals.

SIDS are another vulnerable group of countries. Total external debt stocks of SIDS more than doubled between 2008 and 2017, while GDP increased by just over 30 per cent during the period. Not surprisingly, average debt to GDP ratios also deteriorated across the board, increasing from 28.3 per cent in 2008 to 58.2 per cent in 2017. This left some SIDS facing debt to GDP ratios well above the 100 per cent mark. Public finances have continued to be suffocated by heavy debt servicing costs, which accounted for 16 per cent of government revenue in 2010, and more than doubled to 40 per cent in 2015 before easing to a still high 34 per cent in 2017. SIDS face high levels of environmental risks that make their economies vulnerable to adverse climate events. Successful policy initiatives for SIDS need to tackle environmental and growing debt vulnerabilities to avoid a vicious cycle of growth slowdowns and unsustainable debt burdens.

As a continent, Africa is confronted by a particular dilemma when it comes to debt sustainability, which UNCTAD has highlighted.[24] African countries will have to mobilize significant financial resources to achieve the Sustainable Development Goals and implement the African Union's Agenda 2063. At the same time, the continent must remain vigilant about how it uses and manages such financial resources to avoid spiralling into debt crises. Debt should be incurred if financial resources are channelled into building domestic productive capacities rather than supporting public consumption. In harnessing various development finance resources, African countries will need to strike a balance between increased financing needs and overall debt sustainability.

Despite these ostensibly daunting challenges and the spectre of debt vulnerability, the global South itself has some new financing options (see chapter 4). These and other new sources of development finance from Southern development partners that have emerged can offer a different set of lending conditions from traditional sources. Access to development finance from these Southern development partners involves fewer conditionalities and less stringent information disclosure requirements.

Such borrowing, though, still has to be managed responsibly, whatever the category of vulnerable countries. Strengthening institutional capacities for rating, monitoring and managing debt, whether public or private, is also critical for African countries, as this will help with more sustainable management of their debt levels. In the same line, public–private partnerships – an increasingly popular means to finance infrastructure in Africa, for example – should be managed within

> **Despite the challenges and spectre of debt vulnerability, the global South itself has some new financing options.**

[23] International Monetary Fund, 2018.

[24] UNCTAD, 2016b.

clear legal, policy and regulatory frameworks, underpinned by risk mitigation mechanisms that include provisions for handling contingent liabilities and ensuring debt sustainability.

Multilateral processes are also well under way, not least of which is the forum on financing for development follow-up of the United Nations, led by the Economic and Social Council. As part of the United Nations system, the principles on responsible sovereign lending and borrowing, launched in 2012 by UNCTAD, could be a particularly important tool in promoting debt sustainability in developing countries. Domestic debt, external private debt, debt composition and sovereign debt restructuring are all focus areas of UNCTAD technical assistance to African countries, through development of statistical series and capacity.

CHAPTER 2

South meets South: On the path to 2030

2.1 Achieving the Goals through trade in the global South

South–South cooperation can contribute towards achieving the Sustainable Development Goals through various channels, especially trade, finance and capacity-building. It is well established that trade helps to create the conditions necessary for growth and development. Trade provides the means to overcome constraints posed by small domestic markets and gives countries access to larger external markets, as well as skills, technology and capital, which in turn enable better use of productive resources to catalyse structural transformation. The Sustainable Development Goals implicitly recognize the contribution of trade in many areas, while Goal 17 on the means of implementation does so explicitly.

Under Sustainable Development Goal 17, international trade is defined as a means of implementation, and revitalizing the Global Partnership for Sustainable Development is a critical framework for meeting the 2030 Agenda. For international trade to function as a means of implementation, it is essential to promote "a universal, rules-based, open, non-discriminatory and equitable multilateral trading system under the World Trade Organization" (target 17.10). This is in turn instrumental for the achievement of many other targets related to trade policy, including:

- Target 2.b, on correcting and preventing trade restrictions and distortions in world agricultural markets, including through the parallel elimination of agricultural export subsidies;

- Target 3.b, which covers providing access to affordable essential medicines and vaccines;

- Target 8.a, on increasing Aid for Trade support for developing countries;

- Target 10.a, on implementation of the principle of special and differential treatment;

- Target 14.6, on prohibiting, by 2020, certain forms of fisheries subsidies which contribute to overfishing;

- Target 17.12, on timely implementation of duty-free and quota-free market access for LDCs, as well as the issue of preferential rules of origin.

Meeting these targets would also support significantly increasing the exports of developing countries, in particular with a view to doubling LDCs' share of global exports by 2020 (target 17.11).

The role of an efficient and effective services sector and trade in services is particularly noteworthy. A dynamic services economy and trade can make significant contributions towards sustainable development, as achieving many of the Goals and targets implicitly and explicitly requires efficient, equitable functioning of key services sectors and universal access to infrastructure and essential services. Among those key services sectors are health (Goal 3), education (Goal 4), water and sanitation (Goal 6), energy (Goal 7) and infrastructure and innovation (Goal 9). Several specific targets also refer to services such as telecommunications, access to financial services, sustainable tourism and transport.

Recognizing the development potential of South–South trade, especially on a regional scale, many developing countries in all parts of the world have in fact intensified their efforts to promote regional integration in the South, building on the notion of "developmental integration". This approach to regional integration combines trade liberalization efforts with regulatory and development cooperation on a regional scale, aimed at building productive capacities and improving

Trade gives countries access to larger external markets, as well as skills, technology and capital.

regional infrastructure and connectivity. Several countries have embarked on expansion and revamping of existing South–South regional integration initiatives as a key strategy to support structural transformation in subregional and regional economies. The historic formation of the African Continental Free Trade Area in March 2018 to boost intra-African trade, which built on ongoing subregional and regional integration initiatives, is a vivid example of the approach (see chapter 6).

These initiatives are complementary to multilateralism in international trade and instrumental for revitalizing the Global Partnership for Sustainable Development. This is particularly the case at a time when the heightened risk of "trade war" on a global scale has affected the outlook for multilateral trade cooperation. Greater South–South trade cooperation would allow developing countries to move faster in harnessing the development benefits of trade, where possible, among partners with similar levels of development and, at the same time, can prepare them for subsequent trade integration and cooperation on a multilateral scale.

Another initiative that originated among countries of the South is the Global System of Trade Preferences among Developing Countries, a platform for South–South trade cooperation on an interregional scale that has shown the potential to bring about economic gains (box 2).

> **A key strategy to support structural transformation is expansion and revamping of existing South–South regional integration initiatives.**

Box 2

A global scheme to promote and expand trade in the South

The Global System of Trade Preferences among Developing Countries was created in 1989 as a mechanism for preferential tariff reductions and other cooperation measures to stimulate trade between developing countries. First conceived and developed by the Group of 77, under the auspices of UNCTAD, the scheme's membership currently extends to 43 developing countries. Members include the countries of the Southern Common Market – Mercosur, the first subregional grouping to have acquired full membership, and seven LDCs. Participants aim at promoting economic growth and development by capitalizing on South–South trade.

A third round of negotiations, launched in 2004 at the eleventh session of the United Nations Conference on Trade and Development in São Paulo, Brazil, aimed at broadening and deepening tariff concessions, particularly to promote interregional trade among participants. These negotiations concluded in December 2010 at a ministerial meeting in Foz do Iguaçu, Brazil, with 8 participants (a total of 11 countries, including four member States of Mercosur) adopting the São Paulo Round Protocol under the Global System, amid an exchange in tariff concessions.[a]

The economic significance of the São Paulo round results is reflected in the combined population of the eight signatories – over 2 billion people, accounting for 28 per cent of world population. At the time of signing the Protocol, imports by the 8 signatories were valued at around $1.5 trillion, of which 13 per cent was intra-group trade. In 2015, intra-group imports among the eight signatories (excluding intraregional imports among Mercosur members) stood at some $182 billion. This accounted for 12 per cent of their total imports from the world.

The São Paulo round has the potential to be a milestone in South–South trade cooperation. It is an example of developing countries' ability take the leadership and negotiate an agreement that can creates new trade flows, so as to stimulate trade in a balanced and inclusive manner. To realize that potential, the parties to the Protocol need to complete domestic ratification procedures to secure entry into force of the tariff concessions negotiated. This would be a clear step towards reinvigorating South–South cooperation to drive sustainable development forward. Such a renewed demonstration of political will and engagement in South–South trade could also open the door to expanding coverage and extending cooperation to areas other than tariffs, and even widening participation in the scheme in the long term. Substantive and technical support provided by UNCTAD has been a key contribution to negotiations and towards operationalizing the São Paulo Round Protocol to the Agreement on the Global System of Trade Preferences.

Source: UNCTAD.

[a] The 11 countries are Cuba, the Republic of Korea, India, Indonesia, Malaysia, Egypt and Morocco and Mercosur countries Argentina, Brazil, Paraguay and Uruguay.

2.2 South–South cooperation and Goal 7: Energy[25]

A close look at Sustainable Development Goal 7 provides a specific example of how South–South cooperation can be an effective tool for advancing the 2030 Agenda and achieving the Sustainable Development Goals. Cooperation among developing countries in the global South, and especially with LDCs, can be leveraged to accelerate progress towards Goal 7, on ensuring access to affordable, reliable, sustainable and modern energy for all.[26] Achieving Goal 7 would have the added bonus of positive repercussions for Sustainable Development Goals 1, 5, 8, 9 and 12.

[25] See UNCTAD, 2017b, which is the basis for section 2.2.

[26] Editions of the UNCTAD Least Developed Countries Report series have consistently argued that LDCs are the battleground on which the Sustainable Development Goals will be won or lost, and Goal 7 is no exception.

Figure 4
Access to electricity in the least developed countries, 2014

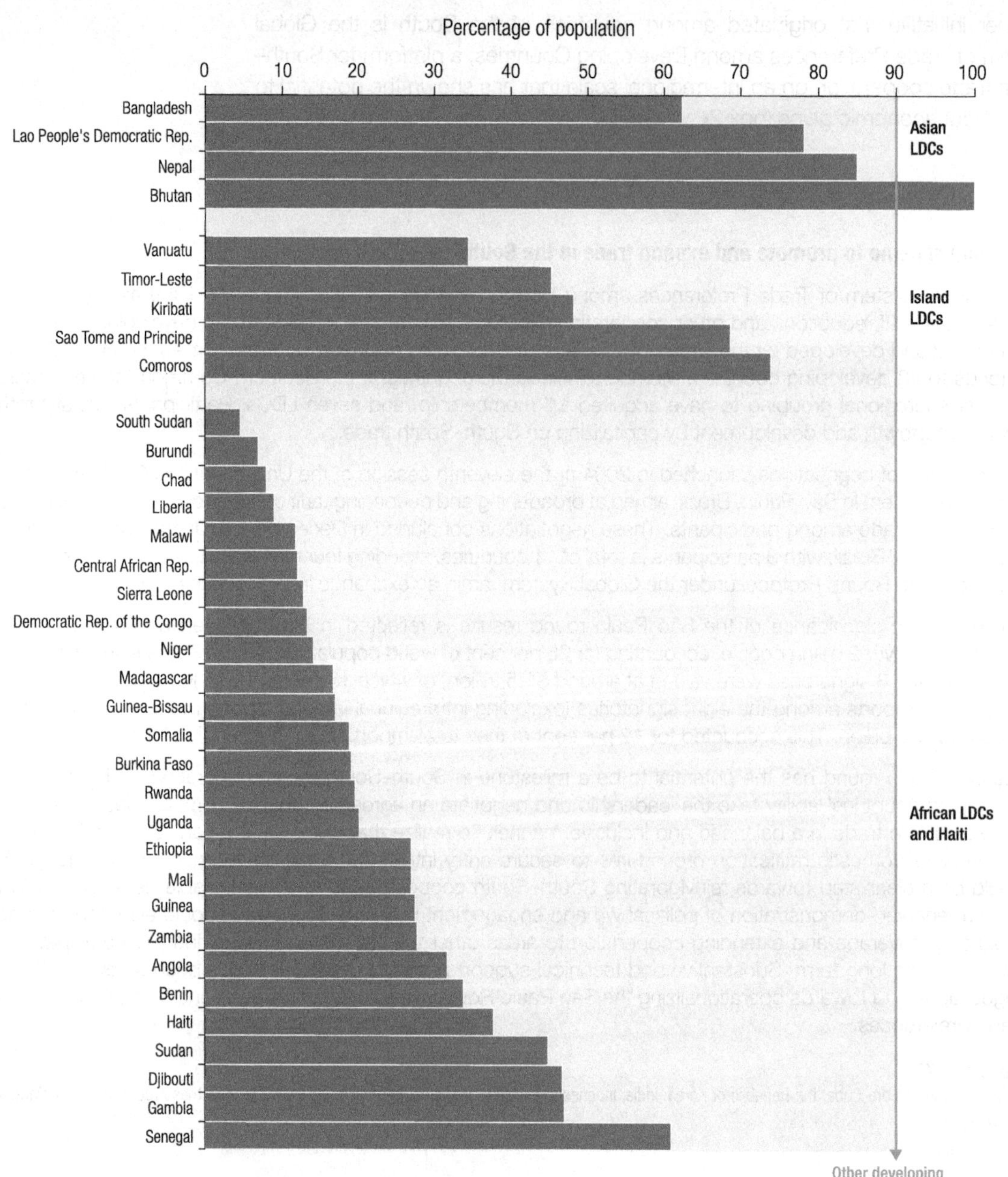

Source: UNCTAD calculations, based on World Development Indicators database (accessed May 2017).
Note: Excludes LDCs for which major discrepancies exist between World Development Indicators and International Energy Agency data.

LDCs made extraordinary progress between 1990 and 2014, more than tripling access to electricity, from 12 per cent to 38 per cent. Yet, this still leaves 62 per cent of people living in these countries without access (figure 4). Achieving universal access to modern energy in LDCS is therefore critical to achieving Goal 7 globally. Energy access in LDCs must be conducive to accelerating structural transformation ("transformational energy access"), going beyond household use and also channelling access to productive uses that support sustained economic growth. However, the financing needs for achieving universal energy access in LDCs by 2030 are enormous, with estimates ranging from $12 trillion to $40 trillion per year. Most of these financing needs must be in the form of long-term finance, given the nature of energy infrastructure projects. South–South financing can make a difference as a source of alternative financing in the context of limited official development assistance from traditional donors and restrained domestic resource mobilization in LDCs. South–South financing is already playing a leading role in energy infrastructure in many countries (see box 3).

South–South cooperation can also be drawn on to increase access to renewable energy technologies, for both households and enterprises in LDCs. Southern-led technology transfers and South–South capacity-building in renewable energy can prove critical. The success of scaling-up of modern energy provision in LDCs hinges on following through on the process of technology transfer. The key would be for LDCs to strengthen national capacities to acquire modern energy technologies and then adapt these technologies to local contexts, to make their integration into national energy systems effective. Technological capability acquisition is all the more critical in the context of the ongoing penetration of renewable-energy technologies, which have witnessed rapid technological advances and whose performance is often determined by site-specific conditions.

Box 3

Alternatives to official development assistance: Looking South

Multilateral development banks in the global South – whether global, regional or subregional in reach – can make use of financial arrangements, instruments and/or terms that differ from traditional institutions. For example, Chinese banks have emerged as global leaders in finance for energy projects in developing countries, and it is estimated that banks and funds of China have doubled the availability of global development finance and hold more assets than the major multilateral development banks operating in developing countries.

In 2015, China announced the creation of the China South–South Climate Cooperation Fund, relevant to the electricity sector. The same year, India also announced a $10-billion concessional credit to African countries over five years, along with $600 million in grant assistance, increasing lines of credit to the continent.

In Africa, China has become the major bilateral source of infrastructure financing. Between 2007 and 2014, Chinese banks added $117.5 billion in energy finance, which doubled the energy financing available globally. The country's dominance in infrastructure finance is expected to continue. China played a major role in capitalizing the New Development Bank and the Asian Infrastructure Investment Bank, which has among its projects approved in 2016 a $20-million electricity generation project in Myanmar and a $165-million project in electricity distribution in Bangladesh.

The scale of lending speaks for itself. The Asian Infrastructure Investment Bank, which began operations in January 2016, is projected to provide $10 billion to $15 billion in loans annually over the next 15 years. It is estimated that the New Development Bank has an annual lending capacity of $3.4 billion by 2024 and almost $9 billion by 2034. Moreover, the Belt and Road Initiative of China[a] calls for large-scale investments in infrastructure and is expected to boost Chinese lending, including in the electricity sector in Asia.

Source: UNCTAD, 2017b.
[a] See section 4.3, chapter 4.

Off-grid technologies (such as Stand-Home Alone Systems) are increasingly regarded as offering a cost-effective solution to the challenge of rural electrification in LDCs. The systems can be deployed faster than grid extension and give rise to a leaner distributed generation model, rather than a centralized one. As this allows rural communities to have access to electricity sooner and supports development of non-farm activities, off-grid technologies also have the potential to promote greater equity and inclusiveness in electrification as well as to offset unsustainable urbanization. A growing number of LDCs are pursuing deployment of Stand-Home Alone Systems under rural electrification programmes, often supported by Southern development partners. It is worth noting that such development partners can be LDCs themselves, namely Bangladesh (which supports deployment with installation subsidies and credit), Rwanda (which has adopted a "rent-to-own" model) and the United Republic of Tanzania.

CHAPTER 3

The power of regions and Southern investment

3.1 When regional is more than global

Global value chains (GVCs) are often considered an indication of the natural evolution of the global trading system and as a promising basis for further trade and investment liberalization (Organization for Economic Cooperation and Development, 2013; UNCTAD, 2013a; World Trade Organization et al., 2013). From a development perspective, GVCs would seem to present an attainable first step towards integrating into global trade and to industrialization. Rather than having to develop an entire product or break into an extremely competitive market on their own, countries can specialize in specific tasks or components of a multitude of value chains, starting at the relatively accessible bottom.

However, the association between participation in GVCs and development is not necessarily positive or a given. UNCTAD research shows that when foreign value added in exports increases and is accompanied by an increase in production and exports of manufactures (as in much of the Asian region, for instance), participation in GVCs by developing countries can complement industrialization and structural change. But when increasing participation in GVCs leads to a reduction of domestic sourcing and domestic value added content in exports, participation in GVCs may lead to delays in structural transformation (UNCTAD, 2016a).

Turning more towards regional markets in the South may offer an alternative. East Asian economies – particularly Taiwan Province of China, the Republic of Korea and Singapore, but also China, despite its global reach in terms of exports and imports – have long recognized the importance of the East-Asian regional production network. Furthermore, in response to the collapse in trade after the financial crisis of 2008/09, a number of developing-country suppliers in other regions shifted their end markets from the North to the South in an effort to regionalize their supply chains. For instance, South African clothing manufacturers moved into other countries in sub-Saharan Africa such as Eswatini and Lesotho, leading to an expansion of the regional value chain (RVC) led by South African retailers (Gereffi, 2014).

RVCs in particular can be instrumental to increasing value added in developing regions. Typically, with RVCs, a country within the given region exports the end product, more often than not to a regional partner, and many activities that add high value are also undertaken within the region. RVCs can therefore significantly contribute to the creation of value at the local level and offer more opportunities to participate, gain experience and build the local capacities needed to compete globally, thus serving as a stepping stone into GVCs (UNCTAD, 2015a). Regional markets might also demonstrate better upgrading potentials, particularly in terms of functional upgrading, including design, marketing, branding and distribution.

Using such a strategy successfully depends, though, on the capacity of developing countries to provide an environment conducive to participation in RVCs and that would make their domestic firms competitive at different points along the RVCs. Successful participation in RVCs also relies on ensuring that the benefits of RVCs translate into domestic development by activating linkages across different productive sectors and eventually reaching most of the population. This in turn requires adoption of a set of ambitious and strategic policy measures at the domestic and regional levels.

Active cooperation among Governments to identify and prioritize entry points into RVCs and exploit regional complementarities, while fundamentally important, often requires coordinating policies across a country's various sectors to avoid having sectors undermine each other. In Southern Africa, for example, use of protective measures in the United Republic of Tanzania (for sunflower oil production) and in Zambia (for soya oil production) may weaken the potential for cooperation between these countries in agro-processing. Facilitating connections between firms operating in different countries at different points of RVCs is equally important. This obviously implies infrastructural investments to curb physical transport costs but also easing border restrictions, harmonizing testing and certification systems and developing regional mechanisms to smooth trade in and setting prices (price discovery) for different commodities.

Governments also need to target actions to ensure that the educational and training system synchronizes the skills provided with the skills needed by the productive sector and favours positioning developing countries at a relatively high level along RVCs. Investment in domestic technological capabilities is of crucial importance in this respect, as is strengthening of cooperation and linkages between research institutes, universities and firms. Where these actions have been put in place, as for example in Scandinavian countries, students receive hands-on experience before entering the labour market through various apprenticeship programmes operated jointly by universities and private companies, joint research projects and knowledge-sharing workshops.

In order to maximize the developmental impact of participation in RVCs, it is also important to take into account the specificities of a given country (and RVC). A vast array of policies can be devised to facilitate the diffusion of benefits associated with participation in RVCs. For example, setting up rapid development zones or free industrial areas in regions where natural resources are concentrated would favour private investment and foster resource exploitation and upstream participation in value chains. This also potentially benefits firms not operating directly in resource extraction.

Finally, it is particularly important to mitigate the potential negative impact of price changes on consumers in low-income households and businesses. The Southern African Development Community, for example, is currently considering the idea of turning consumers into self-producers to promote small-scale, renewable energy-based systems that can contribute to electricity security and equity (UNCTAD, forthcoming).

3.2 Southern investment flows

In general, developing-country multinational enterprises use greenfield projects more often than developed-country multinational enterprises, especially for investment towards recipient developing countries. Between 2007 and 2017, of total greenfield investments made by developing-country multinational enterprises, on average, 80 per cent went to developing countries. By contrast, on average, 50 per cent of total greenfield investments made by developed-country multinational enterprises went to developing countries (figure 5). Therefore, when the South invests in the South, investments directed towards the production capacity of developing countries are also more likely to immediately increase.

Furthermore, most South–South investment occurs intraregionally, sustained by regional markets and RVCs, as well as the relative ease of internationalization in neighbouring economies with which multinational enterprises are familiar. Some factors that explain where multinational enterprises from developing economies decide to invest compared to multinational enterprises from developed economies are historical connections, geography of natural resources and home government policies. In addition, some large outward investors are State-owned and investments reflect the priorities and strategies of the controlling State.

Greenfield investments going to the global South

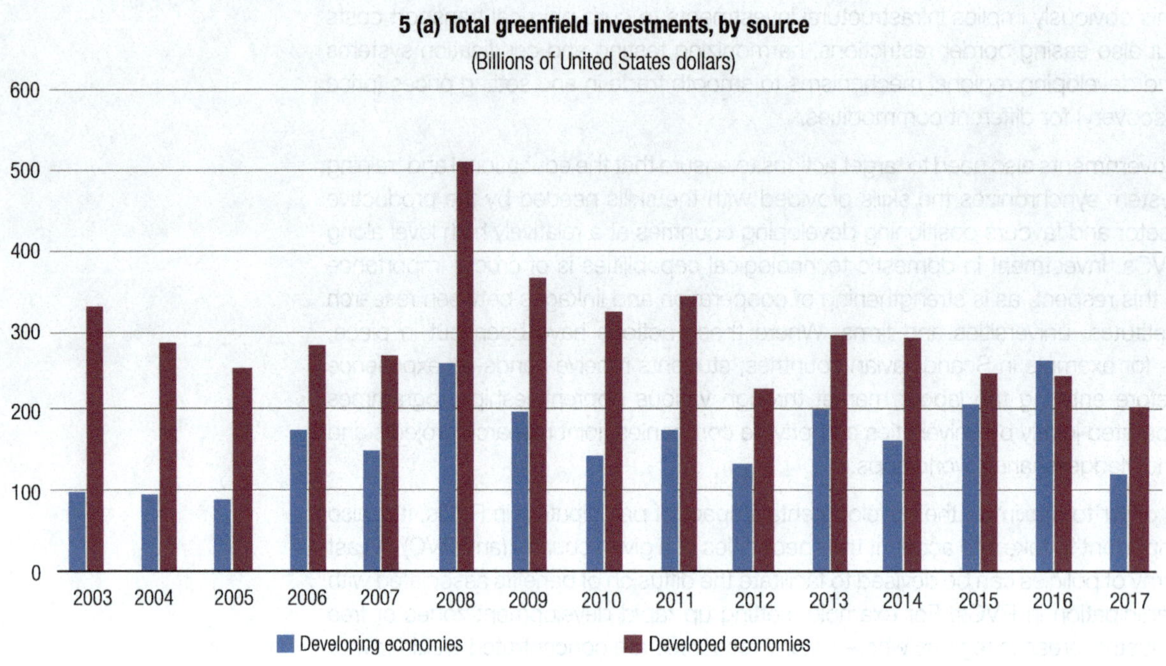

Source: UNCTAD calculations, based on information from the Financial Times Ltd, fDi Markets (www.fDimarkets.com).

The growing and significant international participation of firms from developing and transition economies gives rise to development opportunities for both home and recipient economies. Through outward investment, developing-country multinational enterprises can benefit from market expansion, enhanced efficiency and increased competitiveness. For recipient developing economies, investment from other developing countries can provide a broader range of potential sources of capital, technology and management skills. For low-income developing countries, these benefits can be of great importance. In several LDCs, investment from developing economies accounts for a large share of total FDI inflows.

As the motivations and competitive strengths of developing-country multinational enterprises and the advantage of locations sought by these firms differ in many important respects, their impact on recipient countries may carry certain advantages over that of FDI from developed countries. For example, technology and business models of developing-country multinational enterprises are generally similar to those used by firms in recipient developing countries, which suggests that beneficial linkages and technology absorption are more likely. Developing-country multinational enterprises are also often oriented towards labour-intensive industries and may therefore be inclined to use more labour-intensive technologies, especially in manufacturing. Consequently, they may have greater potential to create jobs in recipient countries.

However, South–South FDI also carries risks. These risks include "crowding-out effects", market dominance issues and, in some cases, relaxed labour and environmental regulations. In some recipient developing countries, these problems are exacerbated by the absence of an adequate regulatory framework.

To boost South–South investment, and magnify its development impact, efforts need to be made by both recipient and home countries. As far as home countries are concerned, increasing numbers of developing countries are dismantling barriers to outward investment, while many of them maintain forms of capital control to mitigate the risk of capital flight or financial instability. Such restrictions are mostly aimed at limiting non-FDI related international capital flows. However, further efforts can still be made by home-country Governments to encourage and facilitate outward investment towards other developing economies. For example, in sectors related to the Sustainable Development Goals, improvements can be made through targeted credit or insurance programmes to encourage investment in agriculture, infrastructure and sustainable energy, as well as RVC development. Meanwhile, home-country measures need to be implemented to encourage responsible investment behaviours of resident international companies to ensure sustainable development impacts benefit both recipient and home economies.

For recipient developing countries, it is important to ensure there is an appropriate investment policy framework to induce greater investment by developing-countries multinational enterprises, while boosting the absorptive capacity of local firms, in the face of new competition from multinational enterprises of other developing countries, through entrepreneurship, technology, skill development and linkages programmes. In addition, good governance and capable institutions are essential to attract investment and maximize its positive impact.

Many of these issues and challenges cannot be addressed by national policies alone. Cooperation at the regional and international levels among developing countries of the global South plays an instrumental role, particularly in investment policy coordination and harmonization.

The investment policy framework outlined in the UNCTAD *Investment Policy Framework for Sustainable Development* (UNCTAD, 2015c) supports investment policy coordination and harmonization, by providing an overarching set of core principles for investment policymaking to guide both national and international investment policy design. This makes the investment policy framework a useful tool for regional investment policy coordination.

There are actions that recipient and home country Governments can take to direct more investment towards supporting the 2030 Agenda, as proposed in the UNCTAD global action plan for investing in the Sustainable Development Goals (UNCTAD, 2015b). One of the action plan's key components – "regional Sustainable Development Goals investment compacts" – calls for strengthened regional cooperation to boost investment in the Goals, which is also naturally

Significant international participation of firms from developing and transition economies gives rise to development opportunities for home and recipient economies.

relevant for South–South cooperation. Specifically, such regional Sustainable Development Goal investment compacts focus on development of regional cross-border infrastructure and of regional industrial clusters to support achieving the Sustainable Development Goals. Broadening the scope of the regional industrial development compacts would present an opportunity to include all policy areas important for enabling regional development, such as harmonization of regulatory standards and consolidation of private standards on environmental, social and governance issues.

Also, many economies interact substantially in RVCs, most of which have a distinctive regional character. At the same time, GVC-based industrialization in developing countries relies on strong ties with the supply base in neighbouring developing economies. This makes cooperation among countries of the South on regional infrastructure and value chain development particularly important and complementary (UNCTAD, 2013a).

Therefore, UNCTAD recommends increased efforts to synergize and strengthen regional collaboration on industrial development, especially in the context of the so-called fourth industrial revolution. Strengthening regional production networks such as border special economic zones or regional corridors are key elements to consider. For example, as seen in one country case study from Argentina, the Government introduced a preferential tax regime for the automotive sector to promote regional car production chains among Mercosur countries (UNCTAD, 2018b).

CHAPTER 4

Financing development from the South

4.1 Development banks and the 2030 Agenda

Reinvigorated
Southern financial
cooperation
has played a
significant role in
a new, emerging
development
finance landscape
in Africa, Asia and
Latin America.

The reinvigoration of South–South financial cooperation since the beginning of the twenty-first century has played a significant role in the emergence of a new Southern development finance landscape, in Africa, Asia and Latin America. Subregional development banks have built on their early successes and scaled up resources for long-term development, while South–South institutions have been established. New development and infrastructure funds have also been created. The China-led Belt and Road Initiative is up and running, already with palpable impacts in both Asia and Africa.

The emergence of this new landscape came at an appropriate time, given that additional sources of finance are needed to support the 2030 Agenda for Sustainable Development. UNCTAD estimated the annual financing gap in key Sustainable Development Goals at $2.5 trillion for the period 2015–030 (UNCTAD, 2014a). Infrastructure development alone, which requires long-term finance for generally large-scale projects, is a critical component for achievement of several Sustainable Development Goals under the 2030 Agenda. Goal 9 is on building resilient infrastructure, promoting industrialization and fostering innovation, Goal 6 emphasizes availability and sustainable management of water and sanitation for all, Goal 7 is on affordable and sustainable energy and Goal 11 covers making cities inclusive, safe, resilient and sustainable. These Goals reflect a few of the types of infrastructure that the 2030 Agenda underscores as critical for realization of key development outcomes in the next 12 years or so.

The outcome of the third International Conference on Financing for Development, known as the Addis Ababa Action Agenda, of July 2015, sought to identify various possible sources of finance and mechanisms to support the Sustainable Development Goals. On international development cooperation, a global infrastructure forum was created to help address the global financing gap in infrastructure development. However, new commitments from the international community for a substantial scaling up of resources have not materialized to the extent needed or expected.

Development banks can serve as effective institutional mechanisms to help finance the Sustainable Development Goals, due to their clear mandate to support development-oriented projects, in-house expertise and track record on identification, development, risk assessment and management of complex projects. Indeed, the Addis Ababa Action Agenda reaffirmed the importance of multilateral development banks as key enabling institutions. A limiting factor is, however, their conservative loan approach and narrow capital base, which constrain their ability to scale up lending significantly. Recently, the World Bank Group announced a capital package that included an increase in paid-in capital to strengthen the Group's financial capacity to support the 2030 Agenda. In addition, the World Bank Group along with the main regional development banks have sought to enhance their lending capacity through balance sheet mergers and optimization. Moreover, they are expanding their tools to leverage private capital for infrastructure and other development-related projects that also fall under the Sustainable Development Goal umbrella.

An area of concern in this new landscape is that low-income countries and many SIDS still need access to concessional financing to help them meet the Sustainable Development Goals of special importance to these countries – for example, Goal 13 on climate action, essential for reducing their vulnerability to climate change-related shocks. Until recently, about 30 per cent of the multilateral development bank loan portfolio was in the form of concessional lending (UNCTAD, 2017c), but this may change in the coming years, because of reforms these banks are undertaking to enhance their lending capacity. These reforms include merging resources in their development funds with ordinary resources, which may adversely affect the level of concessional loans in the future. On the positive side, Southern subregional banks are undertaking new initiatives to raise their own levels of concessional finance. The Development Bank of Latin American (CAF), which does not have a concessional window, is making efforts to obtain softer resources from outside Latin America – e.g. from the development bank, KFW Group, of Germany, and the Global Environment Fund, so that it can support more investment initiatives, especially in green projects, in the region (Development Bank of Latin America, 2018).

More generally, the reality setting in is that of a new dynamism in resource mobilization and scaling up, coming not just from existing Southern institutions, but also from newly created Southern banks. The institutional set-up of the Asian Infrastructure Investment Bank allows it to experiment with a new funding model that has the potential to provide significant sums of development finance, with innovative ideas that can inspire operational improvements in other banks (UNCTAD, 2018b). The BRICS New Development Bank, in turn, has started operations with a clear focus on green projects, which is wholly in line with the need to ensure that the development goals contribute to both inclusive and sustainable outcomes. These banks are also innovating in areas such as governance, funding and partnerships. Their partnerships with other banks include not only co-financing of projects, but also exchange of knowledge and advisory services in priority areas. These partnerships are being established with the large multilateral development banks as well as with subregional and national development banks. The New Development Bank has signed cooperation agreements with global and regional multilateral banks as well as with subregional institutions and national banks. In 2016, the Asian Infrastructure Investment Bank had six of its nine loans for projects co-financed with the Asian Development Bank, the European Bank for Reconstruction and Development and the World Bank (Asian Infrastructure Investment Bank, 2018).

Moreover, the New Development Bank's initial loans have included on-lending operations involving the National Economic and Social Development Bank of Brazil on renewable energy. By partnering with both international and national banks, new Southern banks can become a hub of a worldwide network of development banks, whose main strength resides in diversity of expertise, focus and geographic reach (UNCTAD, 2017c). In this network, national banks can serve as conduits for internalizing and channelling foreign resources for development projects at the national level. Overall, the role of development banks at the regional, subregional and national levels, as summarized above, and the idea such banks can form a worldwide network for supporting the Sustainable Development Goals and development more broadly draws on research UNCTAD has undertaken in the past few years. Figure 6 indicates a new shift to the South that is emerging, in terms of the geographical reach of loans and operational structures that affect banks' member country voting rights (Barrowclough and Gottschalk, 2018; UNCTAD, 2018a; UNCTAD, 2018c).

Development finance: Turning South

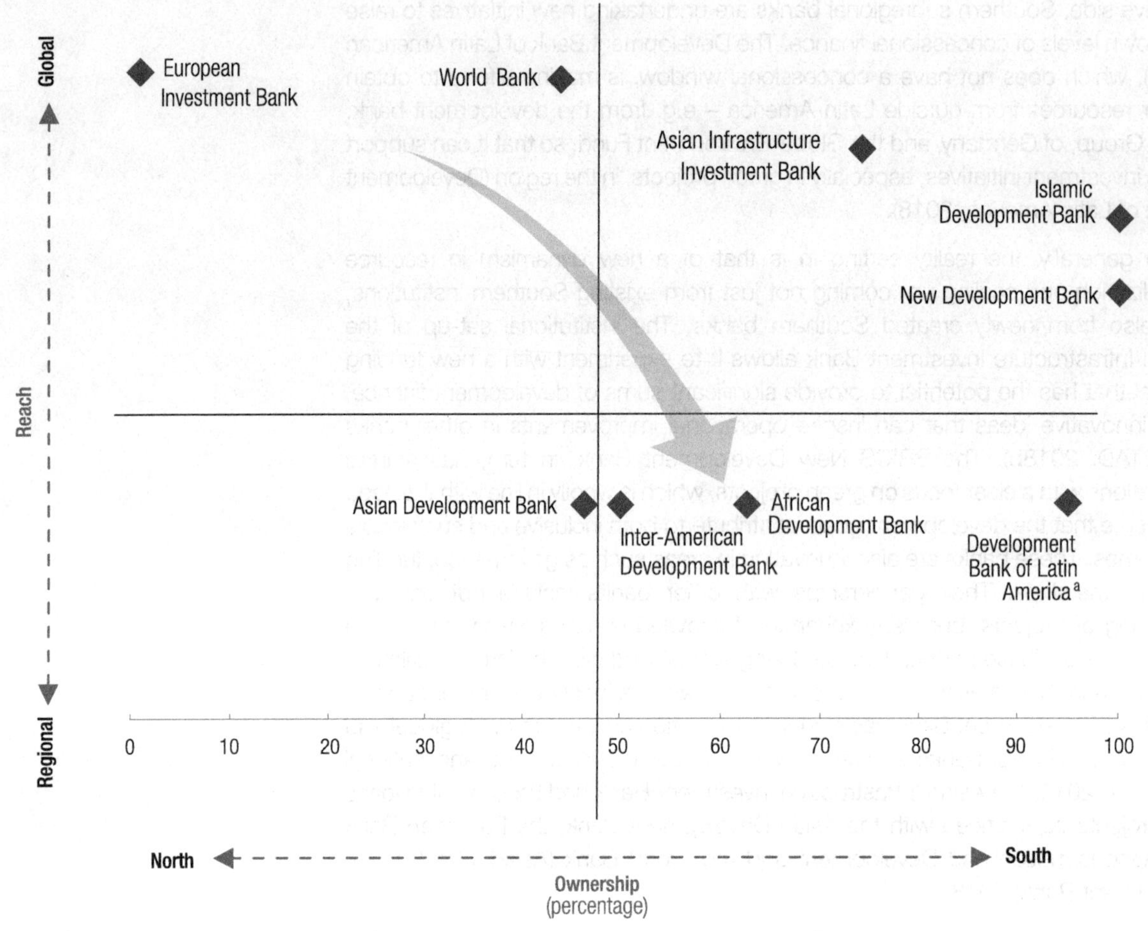

Source: Barrowclough and Gottshalk (2018).
ᵃ Also known as CAF, Andean Development Corporation.

4.2 National development banks: Hidden gems of the South

Development banks with strong abilities to carry out projects at different levels – international, regional and national – can reinforce efforts across levels, especially given large infrastructure deficits in the global South. While the international community is focused on enhancing the lending capacity of existing multilateral development banks, little attention has been given to the role that national development banks could play in boosting development finance and strengthening their ability to execute projects across all phases of infrastructure building. Country experiences with national development banks, however, are not well understood. This subsection briefly summarizes the experiences in some BRICS countries in the interest of South–South policy sharing.

In principle, national development banks are potent policy instruments as they operate in market segments at the heart of the process of structural transformation. Their main function is to address imperfect capital markets that are unwilling to bear the risks associated with extending finance to large-scale capital-intensive projects (or new sectors or products), characterized by high degrees of uncertainty, and long gestation and learning periods. As private investors cannot capture the positive externalities often generated from such projects, leading to underinvestment. National development banks can also be proactive in utilizing their accumulated research, technical expertise and institutional capabilities to shape and create markets, anticipating demand and coordinating domestic supply responses (UNCTAD, 2017c; Hermann, 2010).

In practice, the effectiveness of national development banks as policy instruments has been uneven and their role remains controversial. National development banks carried strong negative connotations in the 1990s and were associated with the excesses of the Asian financial crisis. By the 2008/09 financial crisis, however, as lending from private sector banks dried up, national development banks regained prominence as key sources of long-term countercyclical finance for investment in infrastructure, public facilities and strategic sectors. The 2008/09 financial crisis underscored the enduring importance of development finance, as policymakers began rethinking the role of national development banks in structural transformation and how to effectively wield them (Caixin, 2017; Studart and Gallagher, 2016; Stiglitz and Uy, 1996).

Figure 7 shows broad trends in the role of national development banks in Brazil, China and India, in supporting domestic investment and structural transformation. These rough estimates reveal an increasing domestic role of national development banks in Brazil and China, while that of national development banks of India has stagnated at low levels over the past decade. Individual country experiences are examined below to further underscore the different approaches to using national development banks as part of an overall national development strategy.

The experience of Brazil with national development banks began in 1952 with the creation of the National Economic Development Bank. In the 1960s and 1970s, the National Economic Development Bank was the only domestic source of long-term financing for industry and its contribution to domestic investment grew with the country's industrialization process. The onset of debt crisis and economic stagnation in the 1980s saw the bank's operations fall dramatically from 10.6 per cent to 3.3 per cent of gross fixed capital formation over the 1979–1990 period. The decline in lending, however, was not linear and only dropped to an average of 3.2 per cent in 1989–1990. This can be explained by factors such as: the bank's leading role in supporting the energy sector, including Brazil's ethanol fuel programme in 1979; and expanding the bank's mandate to include agriculture, small and medium enterprises and social programmes. With the focus on social aspects, the bank was renamed the National Economic and Social Development Bank in 1982 (UNCTAD, 2017c; Hermann, 2010).

As Brazil embarked on financial and economic liberalization, the National Economic and Social Development Bank maintained its position in the domestic financial system in the 1990s through its role in preparing firms for privatization and in financing investments by new owners (Hermann, 2010). Funds from privatization sales contribute to funding sources of the National Economic and Social Development Bank, in addition to bond issuance, resources from multilateral organizations, government transfers and compulsory savings mechanisms. By the 2000s, the National Economic and Social Development Bank expanded its international operations, as part of a push for regional integration and in support of firms that were considered "national champions". The bank also played an important counter-cyclical role in the wake of 2008 global financial crisis. However, the bank has been scrutinized for large loans to the country's biggest companies and wealthiest businessmen at subsidized rates (Leahy and

> Little attention has been given to the role that national development banks could play in boosting development finance.

Schipani, 2017). In 2016, for example, large firms received 69.2 per cent of the bank's loan disbursements (National Economic and Social Development Bank, 2017). Moreover, these large firms are generally found in sectors where Brazil has strong comparative advantage (such as food processing and beverages, pulp and paper, and other industrial commodities), rather than in technology- or knowledge-intensive areas that would diversify the economy's competitiveness and skill set (UNCTAD, 2017c).

In China, three national development banks were created in 1994 as part of overall banking sector reforms, as government authorities sought to better distinguish between commercial-based lending and policy-based lending. The three national development banks were the China Development Bank, Export–Import Bank of China and Agricultural Development Bank of China, of which the China Development Bank has the largest balance sheet and a primary focus long-term lending for large-scale infrastructure and industrial projects. Despite initial difficulties, these national development banks were backed by political support and leadership which allowed them an increasingly prominent role at the centre of the country's high-investment growth strategy. In terms of its funding source, the China Development Bank is not a deposit-taking institution and relies instead on borrowing from domestic capital markets rather than direct government support (UNCTAD, 2017c).

Figure 7

Select national development banks: Trends in domestic roles

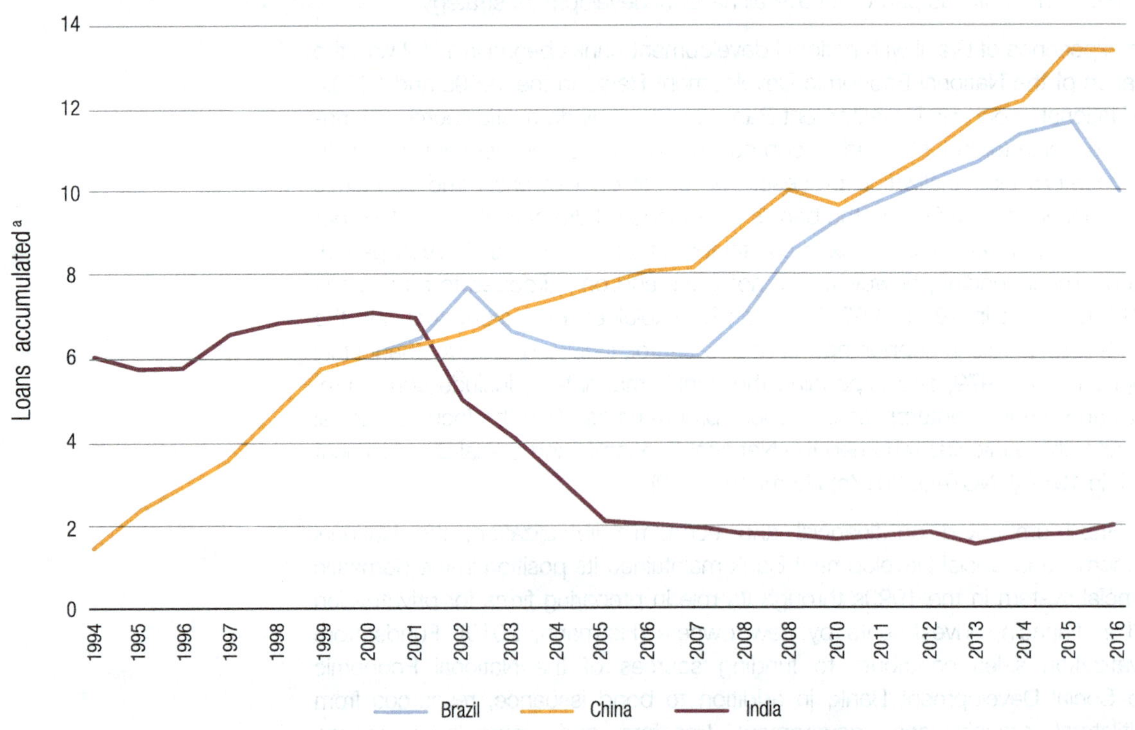

Source: National Economic bords and Social Development Bank of Brazil, financial statements (various years); China Development Bank, annual reports (various years); Xu (2016); Reserve Bank of India Handbook of Statistics on Indian Economy (various years); International Monetary Fund, International Financial Statistics database.

Note: Brazil, includes the National Economic and Social Development Bank; China, includes the China Development Bank; India, includes the Industrial Credit and Investment Corporation of India, Industrial Development Bank of India, IFCI (formerly, the Industrial Finance Corporation of India), National Bank for Agriculture and Rural Development, National Housing Bank, State financial corporations and Small Industries Development Bank of India and Export–Import Bank of India.

[a] As a percentage of GDP.

Plans to place the China Development Bank on a greater commercial footing through measures to bring in an outside strategic investor, take deposits from the public, assume greater responsibility for the risks of its investments, and sell shares in an initial public offering, were halted with the 2008/09 global financial crisis. At the time, local government financing vehicles, pioneered by the bank, played a critical countercyclical role. Since the late 2000s, the China Development Bank and the Export–Import Bank of China have also ramped up the overseas development finance of China and driven export diversification of indigenous technologies in sectors such as renewable energy, telecommunications equipment and transportation (Poon, 2018a). More recently, the country's national development banks, in conjunction with new multilateral development banks (such as the Asian Infrastructure Investment Bank), are backing the Belt and Road Initiative of China – a foreign economic policy focused on building regional infrastructure that could transform South–South relations (Kozul-Wright and Poon, 2015; Dollar, 2018).

The experience of India with national development banks is longer and can be divided into three phases: (a) the late-1940s to mid-1960s; (b) the 1980s; and (c) the late 1990s to early 2000s. The first phase kick-started industrialization, mainly with the creation of long-term nationwide lending institutions: IFCI (formerly, the Industrial Finance Corporation of India) (1948), the Industrial Credit and Investment Corporation of India (1955) and the Industrial Development Bank of India (1964). The 1980s phase featured creation of refinancing and issue-specific institutions, such as the National Bank for Agriculture and Rural Development, National Housing Bank and Small Industries Development Bank of India. In the third phase, however, the country's financial sector underwent major reforms that eliminated development finance institutions' preferential access to concessional government finance and issuance of government-guaranteed bonds (Nayyar, 2015; UNCTAD, 2017c).

These structural changes reduced the role of development finance in India, as major development finance institutions were converted into commercial banks (with the exception of IFCI). Over time, the distinction between providers of short-term finance and long-term finance – associated with development – in the Indian banking system was blurred, which has led to renewed interest in reviving development finance institutions for infrastructure sectors (Reddy, 2017). The country's development finance institutions have historically played a strong role, but major challenges remain insofar as development finance institutions lending was not focused on strategic sectors or on infrastructure, and development finance institutions' relationships with firms often did not extend beyond lending. This lack of coordination between development finance institutions and industrial policy has been attributed to weak institutional control mechanisms. Adequate institutional control mechanisms would adjust incentives according to performance and provide effective checks and balances to prevent and dissuade rent-seeking between Governments and firms or between development banks and firms (Nayyar, 2015).

4.3 The Belt and Road Initiative: An opportunity for supporting the 2030 Agenda

First announced in 2013, the Belt and Road Initiative is a vast foreign economic policy plan of China to enhance cooperation and connectivity in Asia, by financing a wide range of infrastructure projects and productive sector investments. The initiative is conceptualized through the creation of two modern-day "silk roads": the land-based Silk Road Economic Belt and the sea-based 21st-Century Maritime

Silk Road that will stretch across Asia towards Europe. Overall planned investments in countries along Belt and Road Initiative routes are estimated at $900 billion, with over $50 billion invested by China between 2014 and 2016 (Xi, 2017). As part of the financial package announced at the Belt and Road Forum for International Cooperation in 2017, the China Development Bank established loan facilities for Belt and Road Initiative projects totalling RMB 250 billion ($36.2 billion). Of this total, RMB 100 billion is earmarked for loans for infrastructure building, RMB 100 billion is earmarked for "production capacity cooperation" and RMB 50 billion, for financial cooperation (Belt and Road Forum for International Cooperation, 2017).

4.3.1 Infrastructure for the Goals: Southern transport networks

The Belt and Road Initiative is about developing six transport routes[27] running through Asia, Europe and Africa. The Initiative's objectives are: (a) strengthening connectivity, communication and cooperation among Belt and Road Initiative countries and improving (b) policy coordination, (c) trade facilitation, (d) infrastructure connectivity and (e) financial integration. The Belt and Road Initiative intermodal infrastructure network is expected to connect 60 countries, many of which are considered countries with high growth potential (Wang, 2015).

The ambitious Initiative seeks to improve the country's connectivity with the rest of the world. A 10 per cent improvement in connectivity among Belt and Road Initiative countries is estimated would reduce trade costs for China by 3 per cent, increasing the country's imports by 6 per cent and its exports by 9 per cent (Good, 2017). At the national level, the Belt and Road Initiative is also expected to revitalize the country's domestic industries and lead to higher returns for Chinese capital, higher demand for Chinese goods and services, absorption of the country's labour and use of excess Chinese industrial capacity (Zhu, 2015). The expectation is that it will also accelerate development of the country's western region.

The Belt and Road Initiative is likely to have an impact on global transportation networks and trade. For instance, the Maritime Silk Road could have implications for the geography of trade as new opportunities will open for ports and hinterland transport along the new shipping and trade lanes. In addition to maritime routes, by providing surface transport linking Asia to Europe, the Belt and Road Initiative offers alternative logistic options for business and trade, especially for high value added and time-sensitive goods. Optimization of transport infrastructure, services and cross-border trade related processes could help reduce transport costs and thus increase global and regional trade flows.

---

[27] The New Eurasian Land Bridge, China–Mongolia–Russian Federation corridor, China–Central Asia–West Asia corridor, China–Indochina Peninsula corridor, China–Pakistan corridor and Bangladesh–China–India–Myanmar corridor.

Box 4

Cooperation opportunities for transport and trade facilitation reforms

Given its scale and characteristics, the Belt and Road Initiative represents an interesting South–South cooperation opportunity to support transport and trade facilitation reforms linked to achieving several Sustainable Development Goals. The Initiative includes three elements that could contribute to addressing challenges (faced by developing countries) that lead to transport and trade facilitation bottlenecks and can, in turn, affect trade prospects:

a. Significant investments to develop road, rail, ports, logistics and pipeline infrastructure (UNCTAD, 2016d) can contribute to close the persistent infrastructure gap derived from difficulties to scale up financing. Infrastructure investment needs for Asia were estimated at $50 billion a year through 2020 while in Africa these needs were estimated to exceed $93 billion (Bloomberg, 2015).

   China has established the Silk Road Fund (US$40 billion) and the Asian Infrastructure Investment Bank. In 2016, Asian Infrastructure Investment Bank lent US$1.73 billion to support sustainable infrastructure projects related to transport, energy and urban development projects in countries including Bangladesh, Indonesia and Tajikistan (Development Finance, 2017). In 2017, Asian Infrastructure Investment Bank extended loans to 24 infrastructure projects in 12 countries. Total loans amounted to US$4.2 billion, mobilising an additional $17 billion from other public and private investors (Poon, 2018a).

b. The development of economic corridors provides the possibility of fostering value added activities, that can have a positive impact in diversification of Belt and Road Initiative countries. In the context of the Initiative, the six corridors will link central cities and ports along the international routes and industrial agglomerations (promoted via economic industrial parks and free trade zones). The Belt and Road Initiative's economic corridors will cover construction, metallurgy, energy sources, finance, telecommunications, logistics and tourism sectors. Industrial parks are envisaged as cooperation platforms. Free trade zones foresee several trade and investment incentives and trade facilitation measures.[a]

c. Cooperation to support trade facilitation reforms. Trade facilitation is part of the Belt and Road Initiative cooperation agenda under the headline "unimpeded trade". It refers, among other issues, to: regional coordination regarding regulations and procedures (to allow for the flow of goods through multiple jurisdictions); enhanced cooperation on inspection, quarantine, certification and standard measurement; customs clearance formalities; paperless clearance; "single-windows"; best practices in risk management and controls; facilitated procedures in free trade zones and capacity-building (Waters, 2017).

Trade facilitation is an important component of the Belt and Road Initiative. This is because countries along the corridors face complex trade procedures. In the case of landlocked Central Asia, areas of concern include: heavy administrative requirements; difficulties for obtaining mandatory documents; duplication of controls by different agencies; lack of transparency regarding regulatory requirements and discontent with how value declarations are dealt with (ibid.).

Source: UNCTAD.
[a] Shanghai Stock Exchange and Association of Chartered Certified Accountants (2017).

Key areas for South–South cooperation

5.1 Strengthening regional and interregional integration from different fronts

Strengthening regional and interregional integration requires addressing both the 'push' factors that have encouraged developing countries to integrate more closely in recent decades and the 'pull' factors. Both gathered steam in the years following the global financial crisis of 2008/09, but for many developing countries, this simply intensified a trend towards South–South integration that had been proceeding for several decades already. Push factors include the frustrations with the limitations and failures of the global financial architecture and traditional multilateral lenders; the lacklustre economic performance and sluggish demand from northern economies in the post-crisis years; and a reappraisal of developing countries' experience in GVCs and other forms of global trade. As long as the global financial architecture remains unreformed and developing countries do not feel sufficiently supported in times of economic crisis or for long-term development needs, and as long as global trade appears uncertain, then it is to be expected that regional integration will strengthen, if only as a default reaction.

Alongside this, the pull factors that were already encouraging southern regional integration will likely continue, however they need to be better supported in order to be more inclusive and sustainable. For example, one important form of South–South cooperation is the formation of pools of foreign reserves that can be called upon in times of balance of payments crisis (such as the Arab Monetary Fund, the Latin American Reserve Fund or Asia's Chiang Mai Initiative Mechanism). There is a growing interest in these mechanisms especially as gyrating and abruptly reversing short-term capital flows can wreak havoc on developing countries' exchange rates, raising the risk of liquidity shortage and even crisis if countries find themselves unable to service international debt. The Latin American Reserve Fund, for example, aims at being nimble and moves quickly to offer non-conditional loans to its members in times of stress and, as it is a first resort rather than a last, it is a complement to multilateral institutions such as the International Monetary Fund rather than a replacement. It has been called upon almost 40 times in as many years. UNCTAD research and consensus-building activities on these mechanisms in recent years show that these regional arrangements and credit swaps are an increasingly important addition to the international financial landscape (UNCTAD 2018b). Figure 8 underscores that, for the 50 member countries of South–South mechanisms – namely, Latin American Reserve Fund, Chiang Mai Initiative Multilateralization, Arab Monetary Fund and Eurasian Fund for Stabilization and Development, short-term support from their regional arrangements was relied upon 219 times over the years 1976 to 2015, while the International Monetary Fund was used 117 times. More recently, bilateral swaps between Southern countries have been particularly important.

In another complementary approach, Southern countries have come together to try to reduce their vulnerability is through the formation of regional payment systems that reduce their exposure to the gyrations of global foreign exchange markets. The Unitary System of Regional Payment Compensation (SUCRE, by its Spanish acronym) for example, has helped member countries reduce their exposure to exchange rate volatility, and has also lowered the transactions costs of importing or exporting for small and medium-sized enterprises.

However, these payment systems are at best small, and reserve fund groupings do not exist in all parts of the developing world, nor can all members of regional groups be supported at the same time (especially for countries that are very large). Swaps are not an option open to all countries. Hence, it is by no means the case that these arrangements can handle the next big wave of crises. Shocks and

One form of South–South cooperation is the formation of pools of foreign reserves to draw on in times of balance of payments crisis.

Figure 8
Use of short-term loan support from South–South regional arrangements

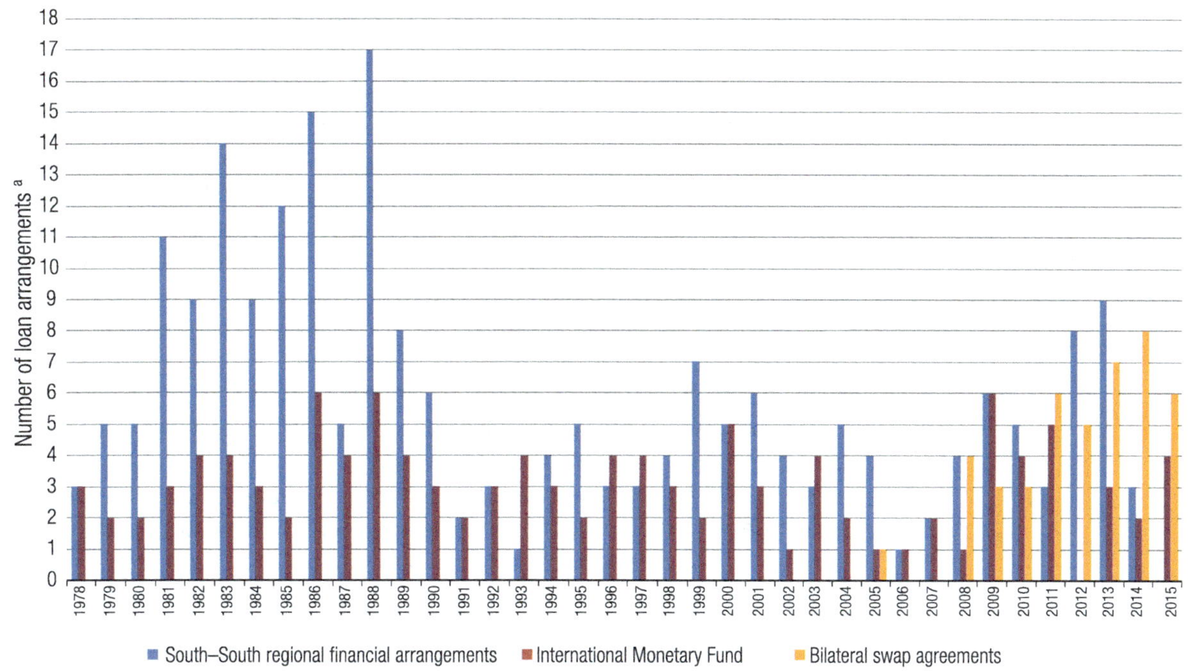

Source: Mühlich and Fritz (2018), in UNCTAD (2018b).
[a] Includes the Latin American Reserve Fund, Chiang Mai Initiative Multilateralization, Arab Monetary Fund and Eurasian Fund for Stabilization and Development.

spillovers can be on a very large scale and highly detrimental; capital reversals and currency fluctuations are driven by global factors out of the control of most national Governments; and the size and degree of interconnectedness of those shocks and spillovers is extreme. Therefore, while the new South–South mechanisms are highly significant and relevant, reform of the multilateral financial architecture and its institutions remains an essential priority in order to meet the needs of all countries (UNCTAD, 2018a).

As described in chapter 4, another important area where support is needed concerns the Southern-oriented and Southern-governed mechanisms for the provision of long-term finance. These are already proving to be an important catalyst for infrastructure and other development projects that were not attracting global investment. However, they need political and financial support so that the many Southern-based national banks already lending to neighbouring countries (such as the National Economic and Social Development Bank of Brazil or the Development Bank of Southern Africa, in South Africa), and the new or expanding Southern-based multilateral banks (such as the Asian Infrastructure Investment Bank or the Islamic Development Bank), can continue their role. At present, many if not most are underfinanced for the task needed, raising the prospect of risky efforts to scale up their lending.

Supporting South–South efforts to boost fiscal capacity and clamp down on tax "caves" will be a big help for this, given the trillions of dollars that are being diverted from developing country Governments; but again, this will also require support at a global level, with regulations that have real teeth. In another vein, support for the South–South flanking policies such as interregional industrial cooperation (e.g. Latin America's pharmaceutical procurement agreement) and cross-border regulation and planning mechanisms for infrastructure are other obvious proactive factors to help strengthening regional integration because they will encourage regional production, consumption and trade. Support for boosting capacity and expertise in national Governments is needed, as well as in financial institutions, in order to help countries better take advantage of the new opportunities that are emerging.

On other fronts. integration among developing regions, especially among African countries, needs to be strengthened. Over the past years, a myriad of initiatives has been put in place to support regional integration in Africa, (e.g. the Action Plan for Boosting Intra-African Trade and the Minimum Integration Programme, backed by the African Union). The various setbacks encountered in the African regional integration process offer policy lessons in the area of strengthening Southern-led regional integration processes. UNCTAD advocates for Africa to rethink its approach towards regional integration, away from away from a linear and process-based approach to regional integration, which focuses mostly on the removal of trade barriers, to a development-based approach, which pays as much attention to the building of productive capacity and private sector development as to the elimination of trade barriers. While the elimination of trade barriers is important, it will not lead to a significant expansion of intraregional trade if productive capacities are not developed. Furthermore, in the African context, there is a need to ensure that the benefits of integration flow to all countries (UNCTAD, 2013b).

Using regional integration to enhance international competitiveness and integrate African countries into global markets is also important. With this vision, there is a need for African countries to promote intra-African trade within the context of developmental regionalism. This requires deliberate government measures to strengthen the domestic private sector and promote industrial restructuring and economic transformation. It also requires a strategic approach to trade policy, coordination of investment into priority areas and strengthening of the institutions and capabilities of African Governments for implementing economic policies. UNCTAD has identified industrial policy, development corridors, special economic zones and regional value chains as important tools and vehicles for promoting intra-African trade within the context of developmental regionalism (UNCTAD, 2013b). Promoting entrepreneurship and building supply capacity are also vital to enhancing the capacity of African enterprises to produce and export goods to regional markets and make the most of regional integration. Efforts to promote entrepreneurship and intra-African trade should address the challenges presented by five distinctive features of Africa's enterprise structure, namely high and rising levels of informality, the relatively small size of African firms, weak inter-firm linkages, low levels of competitiveness and the lack of innovation capability.

Finally, the ongoing ratification of the African Continental Free Trade Area in 2018 marks a milestone towards implementing the vision expressed in the Abuja Treaty back in 1991 to build a single market in Africa (see chapter 6).

5.2 Sustainable and inclusive trade: Removing trade and non-trade barriers in the South

The removal of trade and non-trade barriers among Southern development partners, along with increased freer flow of capital, labour, and services especially through regional trade agreements, can support the building of productive and trade capacities in the South, benefiting LDCs, landlocked developing countries and SIDS. South–South cooperation can be an effective lever for developmental regionalism and the reaping of its benefits.

> **UNCTAD advocates for Africa to consider shifting to a development-based approach to regional integration.**

Adopting a "developmental regionalism" approach, in which regional integration is used to build an industrial base and address supply-side constraints to private sector development with the aim of improving international competitiveness, holds much promise for some Southern regions such as Africa. It is argued that to meet the key challenge of economic transformation, regional integration initiatives need to be designed and carried out within a broader development framework, which promotes economic diversification, structural transformation and technological development, thereby enhancing the productive capacities of African economies, realizing economies of scale, facilitating infrastructure development and supporting industrialization. This in turn leads to increased foreign and domestic investment, enhanced trade, improved competitiveness and development of human capital. In this way, Africa will be able to attain high, sustainable and shared economic growth and become further integrated into the global economy (UNCTAD, 2013b).

Box 5 shows how UNCTAD supports increasing transparency and regulatory cooperation on non-tariff measures in regional and South–South partnerships.

Box 5

Cooperating across the South on non-tariff measures

Non-tariff measures affect our lives every day. Nowadays, over 80 per cent of global trade is affected by such regulatory non-tariff measures. Regulatory measures are indispensable and crucial for sustainable development. Still, non-tariff measures also raise consumer prices and create hurdles to trade and economic development. UNCTAD estimates show that the aggregate impact of non-tariff measures is three times higher than tariffs. Furthermore, non-tariff measures disproportionately and negatively affect smaller countries and producers. UNCTAD supports increasing transparency and regulatory cooperation on NTMs in regional and South–South partnerships.

In the Association of Southeast Asian Nations (ASEAN), UNCTAD collaborates with all member States and the Economic Research Institute for ASEAN and South East Asia (ERIA) to enhance transparency and understanding of non-tariff measures to better cope with their complexity. The information is freely available online and used by diverse stakeholders. ASEAN member States have included UNCTAD–ERIA non-tariff measures data in their strategic action plan for the ASEAN Economic Blueprint 2025 to strengthen their regulatory cooperation and deepen regional integration. Ministers at the 49th ASEAN Economic Ministers Meeting in September 2017 expressed appreciation for the UNCTAD–ERIA non-tariff measures database and agreed that ASEAN member States should "continue… verifying and regularly updating the ASEAN non-tariff measures in the ERIA–UNCTAD non-tariff measures database, examining possible policy options for addressing [non-tariff measures]".

UNCTAD is also supporting the African Tripartite region of the Southern African Development Community (SADC), the Common Market for Eastern and Southern Africa (COMESA) and the East African Community (EAC). Recognizing that the lack of regulatory transparency is contributing to high trade costs, the tripartite regional economic communities requested UNCTAD assistance for the collection of non-tariff measures data in 12 pilot countries. Providing better access to information for policymakers and the private sector promotes trade of developing and least developed countries in the region (target 17.11 of Sustainable Development Goal 17). Data collection has been now completed in most countries, and national validation workshops in Botswana, Malawi, Mauritius, Uganda, the United Republic of Tanzania and Zimbabwe brought together 10 to 20 agencies from each country. The workshops increased inter-agency coordination on non-tariff measures and contribute to policy coherence (Goal 17, target 17.14). The non-tariff measures data are being integrated into the existing tripartite non-tariff barriers reporting, monitoring and eliminating mechanism.[a]

Further UNCTAD-supported regional initiatives on transparency in and cooperation on non-tariff measures focus on the Economic Community of West African States (ECOWAS), the Latin American Integration Association, Mercosur and Pacific island States in the Pacific Agreement on Closer Economic Relations Plus. All regional initiatives also feed data into the UNCTAD global Trade Analysis and Information System.[b] Under UNCTAD leadership, collaboration with these regional partners and international organizations, such as the International Trade Centre, World Bank and World Trade Organization, has successfully increased the availability of non-tariff measures data that now covers more than 90 per cent of world trade.

Source: UNCTAD.

[a] www.tradebarriers.org.

[b] http://trains.unctad.org.

5.3 Cooperating to build trade and productive capacities: Case studies

Landlocked developing countries could gain significantly from regional trade with their neighbours and from global trade if they are to address transport and transit facilitation infrastructure deficits through South–South cooperation within a developmental regionalism approach. South–South cooperation in designing, implementing and financing regional infrastructure projects can help to address competitiveness constraints among Southern landlocked developing countries and make their efforts at building productive (and entrepreneurial) capacities more economically viable. For example, Ethiopia relies heavily on its next-door neighbour, Djibouti, to gain commercial access to the seas and stands much to benefit from the development of efficient logistics in Djibouti to make its exports more competitive on global markets. Cooperation between Ethiopia and Djibouti in investing on common road infrastructure stands to benefit both countries' economies and their trade, growth and economic integration prospects.

Ethiopia needs a trade policy and an efficient and reliable transport and logistics network if it is to meet its Growth and Transformation Path II targets which include an expansion in the manufacturing sector, value addition in all productive sectors and a threefold increase in values of exports. Currently opportunities created by low cost inputs (labour and energy) are cancelled out by factors relating to trade logistics. For instance, labour costs of making a T-shirt in Ethiopia are one third the costs in China, but logistics costs make the T-shirt the same price at market. The country's growth strategy has been driven by a massive public investment programme reaching almost one quarter of GDP by 2014 and accounting for around half of all growth in the economy since 2011. Spending on roads has been about 4 per cent of GDP every year over the last five years and the Ethiopia–Djibouti Standard Gauge Railway has cost Ethiopia about US$3.3 billion. However, without this expenditure on logistics infrastructure there would be limited scope to improve logistics and without improved logistics, Ethiopian manufacturers and other producers will not be price competitive in most regional and international markets. In effect, the Ethiopia–Djibouti Corridor is the only commercial access Ethiopia has to the seas.

The port of Djibouti has, since 1998, handled almost all maritime traffic of Ethiopia. To accommodate this, the port has invested in providing trade and transit facilities, important components of the economy. Djibouti has invested about US$0.8 billion in the Standard Gauge Railway that links with the Ethiopian section to Addis Ababa and has also invested heavily in new port infrastructure, having invested in the Doraleh Container Terminal and are a minor shareholder, and in the Doraleh Multi-Purpose Port as the main shareholder and manager. With the railway and new port facilities in Djibouti, Ethiopia will be able to channel more cargo through Djibouti and Djibouti will be able to handle this additional traffic.

UNCTAD is currently supporting Ethiopia and Djibouti to further improve the logistical performance of the section of the Djibouti–Ethiopia corridor that links Addis Ababa with Djibouti City and the ports of Djibouti.

The Greater Mekong region in Asia is another example of South–South cooperation within a developmental regionalism paradigm, that has helped Southern countries to build their trade and productive capacities. Regional development banks, such as the Asian Development Bank, have a critical role to play in facilitating infrastructure finance in that context.

UNCTAD is currently supporting Ethiopia and Djibouti to improve logistical performance of the Djibouti–Ethiopia corridor.

In 1992, the six countries sharing the Mekong River in South-East Asia – Cambodia, China, the Lao People's Democratic Republic, Myanmar, Thailand and Viet Nam – launched a subregional programme of economic cooperation with the assistance of the Asian Development Bank in order to promote development in the subregion by enhancing economic linkages across their borders. The underlying strategy of this initiative, known as the Greater Mekong subregion economic cooperation programme, was to integrate the countries of the subregion through improvements in infrastructure, with an initial focus placed on overcoming barriers to physical connectivity within the subregion, thereby promoting trade and investment and stimulating economic growth. At the same time, the countries of the subregion agreed on the need for subregional cooperation on other sector issues in order to complement national efforts. Since its inception, the programme has thus adopted a developmental regionalism approach to integration by focusing on infrastructural development and sectoral policy coordination in several areas of cooperation (including agriculture, energy, the environment, human resource development, telecommunications, transport and tourism), as well as promoting cooperation in the cross-cutting areas of trade and investment (UNCTAD, 2013b).

5.4 Sustainable South–South investment

5.4.1 Harmonizing regional investment policy

How South–South regional investments policies are implemented, whether through regional investment agreements or regional/continental free trade agreements, can either help consolidate a regional investment policy regime or create further complexities and inconsistencies. Regional South–South investment agreements have been proliferating in recent years, especially in Africa.

Recent relevant examples of South–South regional investment agreements include: the ASEAN Comprehensive Investment Agreement (2014), which consolidated the 1998 ASEAN Investment Agreement and the 1987 ASEAN Investment Guarantee Agreement; the SADC Protocol on Finance and Investment (as amended in 2016); and the COMESA Common Investment Area (2007), currently under review. There are also South–South investment instruments, models and guidelines, such as the Pan-African Investment Code (2016); the SADC Model Bilateral Investment Treaty template (2012) and the Joint African, Caribbean and Pacific Group of States–UNCTAD Guiding Principles for Investment Policymaking (2017). These examples are in addition to ongoing negotiations for investment provisions within the context of the Tripartite COMESA–EAC–SADC Free Trade Agreement, as well as the African Continental Free Trade Agreement.

These South–South initiatives offer opportunities to consolidate today's multifaceted and multilayered treaty network that currently consists mostly of a patchy network of outdated bilateral investment treaties that were finalized in the 1980s, 1990s and early 2000s. However, consolidation of the treaty network will not automatically confer benefits and particular attention must be made to not create new inconsistencies resulting from overlaps with existing agreements (UNCTAD, 2014a). Where regional investment agreements do not entail the replacement of older bilateral investment treaties the result is the multiplication of treaty layers, further complicating the network of international investment obligations that are already prone to overlap and inconsistency. More specifically, regional investment agreements can create new and different investment obligations on top of existing requirements. Caution must be given as these new agreements may increase the risk of "treaty shopping" by investors looking for the most favourable clauses from different treaties using broadly drafted most-favoured nation provisions.

For South–South regionalism to rationalize the current international investment policy regime and tailor a more coherent, manageable and development-oriented set of investment policies, the relationship between new regional investment agreements and existing bilateral investment treaties between the parties must be clarified and harmonized. However, currently most regional agreements are either silent on the relationship with existing outdated bilateral investment treaties or maintain their existence in parallel. This is despite the potential of these South–South regional investment agreements to supersede a substantial number of older bilateral investment treaties, thereby creating a less convoluted set of international investment obligations that becomes easier to manage. For example, an investment chapter in the African Continental Free Trade Agreement has the potential to replace the 169 intra-African bilateral investment treaties in existence today.

In terms of content, most regional South–South initiatives follow an UNCTAD road map (UNCTAD, 2015b), which sets out five action areas: safeguarding the right to regulate, while providing protection; reforming investment dispute settlement; promoting and facilitating investment; ensuring responsible investment; and enhancing systemic consistency) or include clauses that were set out in the UNCTAD Investment Policy Framework for Sustainable Development (UNCTAD, 2015c) and the UNCTAD reform package for the international investment regime (2017d).

This indicates that while South–South regional investment cooperation represents an opportunity to consolidate and improve the efficiency of the investment policy regime, and improve discrete linkages to sustainable development objectives, regional investment cooperation also presents challenges and complications. It is within this context that developing countries, who are a party to regional investment agreements that include modern sustainable development-oriented provisions, need to consider the pros and cons of maintaining their existing outdated bilateral investment treaties. Therefore, it is crucial for developing countries to synchronize reform efforts at the regional level of policymaking. This requires coordination and cooperation among developing countries and their regional economic integration groups to avoid overlap, policy inconsistencies and fragmentation.

In doing so, and in view of strengthening the sustainable development dimension of their international investment agreement regimes, including with regards to fostering policy coherence, developing countries could consider reviewing their international investment agreement regimes at the bilateral and regional levels, drafting a new model international investment agreement and concluding new generation treaties (phase 1 of reform) as recommended in the UNCTAD road map for international investment agreement reform (UNCTAD, 2015b). Countries may also wish to embark on the reform of their existing and outdated stock of international investment agreements (phase 2 of reform), as recommended in the 10 options of UNCTAD for modernizing the existing stock of old-generation treaties (UNCTAD, 2017d); and finally ensure coherence between their UNCTAD regime, national investment laws and other bodies of law (phase 3 of reform), as recommended in the UNCTAD *World Investment Report 2018*. The three reform phases have been consolidated in a forthcoming reform package for the international investment regime to be released by UNCTAD.

5.4.2 Responsible and sustainable stock exchanges

Sustainable and responsible investment has become a prominent topic for the portfolio investment community. This rise in prominence is exemplified by the rapid growth of the United Nations Sustainable Stock Exchanges Initiative

(SSE), a United Nations partnership programme lead by UNCTAD. The SSE now includes 75 stock exchange members from around the world that are committed to promoting improved environmental, social and governance practices among the companies listed on their exchanges including the promotion of green finance, gender equality and disclosure.

The majority of SSE partner exchanges are from developing countries and are engaged in SSE activities designed to promote South–South learning. Many developing countries face challenges promoting good corporate environmental, social and governance practices impeding to new investment as the international investment community increasingly incorporates environmental, social and governance issues into their portfolio allocation decisions.

The SSE acts as a peer-to-peer learning network, helping to facilitate the exchange of good practices on responsible investment between different countries, especially developing countries. South–South cooperation between stock exchanges and securities regulators who are part of the SSE network helps to accelerate the adoption of proven concepts and practices related to responsible investment. SSE activities include regional roundtables to promote South–South dialogue as well as the organization of study tours between developing countries to exchange information between stock exchanges and securities regulators on sustainable finance. The SSE also provides technical advice to regional exchange associations on responsible investment and sustainable finance. The Association of Securities Exchanges of Africa, for example, recently launched its own sustainability working group, with support from the SSE, to facilitate increased South–South learning on environmental, social and governance issues.

The promotion by the SSE of South–South dialogue and cooperation on responsible investment has played an important role in building consensus around the implementation of environmental, social and governance practices and driven concrete actions on the ground. For example, in September 2015, when the SSE launched its model guidance for stock exchanges, less than one third of stock exchanges around the world provided guidance on reporting environmental, social and governance information for their market. Since then, the SSE has launched a global campaign to encourage exchanges around the world to introduce guidance on environmental, social and governance disclosure. By 2018, the number of exchanges with guidance had more than doubled, with others voicing commitments to the SSE to introduce guidance in the near future (box 6).

Figure 9

Results and impact: Environmental, social and governance guidance campaign
(Number of stock exchanges)

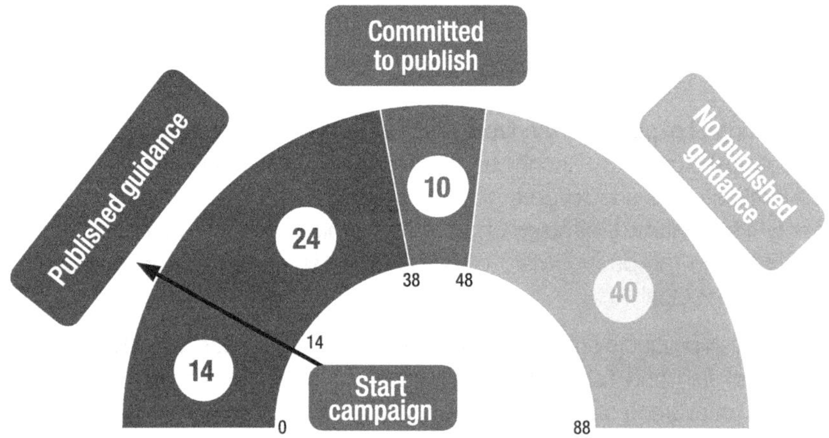

Source: UNCTAD.

> **Box 6**
> **What people are saying about the reporting guidance campaign**
>
> "The Nairobi Securities Exchange commends the United Nations Sustainable Stock Exchanges initiative for championing the development of the model guidance on [environmental, social and governance] reporting globally. Over the following months of 2016, the [Nairobi Securities Exchange] intends to use the SSE model guidance as a basis for the formulation of its own voluntary guidance in consultation with all market players. This will further entrench our commitment to develop sustainable capital markets that will enhance long term value for both our domestic and international stakeholders." – Mr. Geoffrey Odundo, Chief Executive, Nairobi Securities Exchange
>
> "Having voluntarily joined the SSE initiative, Hanoi Stock Exchange deeply acknowledges the importance of issuers' transparent [environmental, social and governance] reporting. With reference to the SSE model reporting guidance, we intend to introduce a roadmap for application of our own customized market guidance on [environmental, social and governance] reporting for listed companies within 2016. We look forward to the good impact of the guidance on enhancing the quality of listed companies, making our domestic securities market more sustainable and attractive to global investors." – Hanoi Stock Exchange
>
> "The voluntary model guidance that is being released by SSE is a good example of how to orientate companies in a didactical and clear way. We congratulate SSE for this initiative. It is an honour to be part of it." – Sonia Favaretto, Sustainability Officer, at B3 (Brazilian Stock Exchange)
>
> *Source*: UNCTAD.

Key success factors learned from the SSE include:

- Close cooperation with partners in developing countries;

- Focus on efficiently connecting relevant organisations in different markets;

- Recognizing programmes in one market might be suitable for another market;

- Providing platforms for sharing experiences and documenting key lessons learned.

Scaling up South–South cooperation can be facilitated by employing both regional approaches and global approaches. Sometimes lessons learned are most relevant for regional neighbours, but in other cases, the most appropriate application of a lesson may be in a country in a completely different region. Scaling up actions to promote South–South cooperation can also be advanced by engaging more closely with existing institutions in the South that were designed for this purpose, but which can benefit from United Nations resources and expertise.

5.5 Experiences of cooperation in the South: Sustainable fisheries and green exports

The sharing of experiences and resources among Southern development partners to facilitate the building of technical, regulatory and institutional capacities in specific economic sectors should be a growing area of South–South cooperation in the twenty-first century. Examples of such economic sectors relates to the Oceans economy and the development of sustainable fisheries, in line with Sustainable Development Goal 14.

Fish and fish products are an important sector of global trade. In 2013, total world exports of fish and fishery products were estimated to reach US$136 billion, showing an average of 12 per cent annual increase over the prior 10 years. Most of these exports are driven by the demand in developed countries, which account for more than 75 per cent of global fish imports. It is anticipated that demand from Asia will grow at a rate comparable to that of demand from developed country markets.

It is important to highlight that LDCs have comparative advantages in fishery resources. Of 16 top inland waters fishery producers, six are LDCs. Overall, in 14 of the current 47 LDCs, fishery exports are ranked in the top five merchandise exports. Despite the significant potential that fisheries hold for socio-economic development, the fishery sector in LDCs is predominantly traditional or artisanal. While many developing countries have substantially increased their share in world fishery exports, from 34.6 per cent in 1981 to 50.2 per cent in 2013, the share of LDCs has risen marginally, from 1.6 to 3.5 per cent in the same period. The sector remains informal, untapped or underdeveloped, facing interacting supply-side and demand-side constraints.

Marine fisheries are also particularly important in SIDS for income generation and for the livelihoods of many coastal communities. Fish exports of SIDS represented about 1.7 per cent of their total GDP in 2012. In some SIDS, fisheries can contribute 10 per cent or more of GDP and may account for up to 90 per cent of animal protein in their populations' diet, with national fish consumption as much as four times higher than the global average per capita.

UNCTAD research shows evidence from selected LDCs in Africa and Asia of a series of supply-side and demand-side challenges undermining the role of the fishery sector in LDCs (UNCTAD, 2017e). SIDS and LDCs can stand to gain from South–South cooperation in their quest to develop their Oceans economy (see chapter 6, section 6.2).

South–South cooperation can also serve as a catalyst to boost greener trade in support of sustainable development. UNCTAD national green export reviews have found that as household incomes in developing countries rise, South–South trade of green consumer products may well be a more successful endeavour than South–North trade, and therefore, greater efforts should be placed on integrating developing country markets addressing tariff and non-tariff measures affecting green products, accompanied by mutual recognition agreements for green product standards. National green export reviews have been implemented in over 10 countries, including Angola, Ecuador, Ethiopia, Lebanon, Madagascar, Morocco, Oman, Republic of Moldova, Senegal and Vanuatu, and focused on green consumer goods selected by national stakeholders, such as organic food, natural cosmetic and sustainably produced fish and forestry products, and green services, such as ecotourism. This shows the importance of strengthening cooperative efforts among developing countries to collectively address sustainability challenges based on the sharing of national experiences, twinning arrangements and South–South training exercises.

> **Sharing of experiences and resources among Southern development partners should be a growing area of South–South cooperation.**

CHAPTER 6

UNCTAD success stories and "champions"

6.1 South–South cooperation on the ground

South–South cooperation is an important feature of many of technical cooperation projects.

UNCTAD has been delivering technical cooperation on trade, investment, finance and technology to support developing countries in achieving nationally and internationally agreed development goals. Over the last 16 years alone, some 130 countries have benefited from UNCTAD technical cooperation. Structurally weak and vulnerable countries (e.g. LDCs, landlocked developing countries, SIDS) are prioritized beneficiaries in UNCTAD technical cooperation. South–South cooperation is an important feature of many of technical cooperation projects. It provides a viable channel for accessing alternative finance and affordable technology, sharing innovative development experience, deepening regional integration and expanding RVCs. To showcase the importance of South–South cooperation in UNCTAD technical cooperation, this section presents a few success stories.

6.2 Cooperation for efficient and effective customs processes

An efficient and effective customs administration is essential to the welfare of any country. It benefits the national economy by: collecting revenue; promoting cross-border trade and combating fraud and illegal trafficking of prohibited and restricted goods. It provides statistical information on foreign trade transactions, essential for economic planning, and encourages international trade.

The Automated System for Customs Data – ASYCUDA – of UNCTAD is an information and communications technology (ICT)-based customs management system to reform customs clearance processes of developing countries. It computerizes and simplifies procedures. ASYCUDA has a major impact on electronic business and government transactions, making international trade simpler and cheaper, and international markets more accessible to enterprises from developing countries.

Customs reform and modernization is a complex endeavour entailing challenges, particularly for developing countries who have limited resources, due its cost and the fact that it requires continuous training and skills updating. The Pacific region, which includes several LDCs (Kiribati, Solomon Islands, Tuvalu and Vanuatu), faces this challenge. In 1998–1999, with financial aid from the Australian Agency for International Development, UNCTAD executed a multi-country customs automation project to deploy ASYCUDA++ in Fiji, Samoa and Vanuatu to support improved trade competitiveness.

Ensuring national administrations can maintain and operate the system independently is a hallmark of ASYCUDA projects. At a time when IT and computer skills were at a premium, the project in the Pacific faced the challenge of trained and qualified staff migrating to developed countries to seek better opportunities, which jeopardized the customs modernization initiative.

To address the challenge of "brain drain" and sustainability, a Memorandum of Agreement was signed in 2002 between Fiji, Samoa, Vanuatu and UNCTAD to set up and operate the ASYCUDA Support Mechanism for the Pacific (ASMP). Papua New Guinea and the Solomon Islands joined the ASMP in 2008 and 2016. The ASMP office is located in Fiji and is managed by a Support Coordinator, who is a staff member nominated by one of the member administrations on a rotational basis.

ASMP is an excellent example of South–South cooperation as it entails:

- 100 per cent funding of operations by developing countries (i.e. ASMP participating countries), through a cost-sharing arrangement;

- An in-built mechanism for capacity-building, given that the rotating responsibility as Support Coordinator of the ASMP office, has (a) enhanced the regional capacity in providing technical support; (b) developed regional management skills for customs reforms; and (c) improved cooperation among customs administrations in the region;

- Training: each administration sends one of their staff to the ASMP office for a period of 15 weeks to undergo a specialized training activity to address specific needs of the nominating administration (fellowship programme). In addition, annual functional and technical trainings are also conducted under the ASMP.

As a specific example, in 2017 the Solomon Islands Customs and Excise Division collected more than SI$1 billion in revenue for the first time in history. This milestone was reached three years after the Government started working with UNCTAD to modernize clearance and revenue collection procedures.

In its 17 years of operation, ASMP has built a pool of regional experts that UNCTAD has tapped to assist other customs administrations in the Pacific. Some of the alumni of the ASMP coordinator and fellowship programmes have been recruited by UNCTAD to provide technical support to the member administrations and to conduct feasibility studies to deploy ASYCUDA in Kiribati, the Marshall Islands, Tonga and American Samoa.

South–South cooperation within the framework of the ASMP has enabled developing countries to take full ownership of modernized and automated customs operations and empowered customs administrations to provide technical support in the region to streamline customs processes and bring about good governance.

6.3 Building least developed country capacities to expand fishery exports

Many LDCs are among the largest producers of fish in the world. Six of the top 16 producers of fish from inland waters are LDCs. The fisheries sector in these countries also contributes to a large share of employment and protein intake and holds significant potential for poverty reduction. Even in landlocked least developed countries such as Uganda, the socioeconomic contribution of fishery is enormous. For Uganda, fish exports are the second largest foreign currency source, after coffee. However, globally, not a single LDC features in the list of the top 10 fishery exporters. Consequently, their combined share in global exports remains marginal at 2 per cent.

UNCTAD has been assisting LDCs to better harness the trade and development potential of the sector to make progress towards the Sustainable Development Goals. It has been implementing a United Nations Development Account project, entitled "Building the Capacities of Selected LDCs to Upgrade and Diversify their Fish Exports", since 2014. The project covers five beneficiary countries, namely Cambodia, the Comoros, Mozambique, Myanmar and Uganda. As part of the project activities, UNCTAD organized technical and policy level training seminars/ workshops in all countries covered by the project as well as regional and interregional experience sharing workshops. These activities helped in creating awareness and revamping regulations and institutions to meet international standards. UNCTAD

> "ASYCUDA has actually facilitated trade – it has helped us in the region to connect… When we shifted from manual to automated, the revenue increased, and it has continued to increase since then. Tax collection has risen too… The extra revenue has helped the island States to finance ASYCUDA themselves."
>
> – Director of the Customs and Inland Revenue Service of Vanuatu

also undertook research and policy analysis, which led to formulating a manual to assist the countries in diversifying and upgrading their fishery exports. The manual has already been translated into several languages including into French, Khmer, Burmese and Portuguese.

South–South cooperation is a prominent feature of this project. As a follow-up to capacity-building activities at the country level, an interregional workshop was organized in Mauritius in April 2017. The same year, regional training workshops in Myanmar (for the Asian region) and Mozambique (for the African region) were also organized. The regional and interregional workshops brought together project countries from Asia and Africa as well as other successful countries, such as Viet Nam, and enabled the sharing of experiences, best practices and knowledge. Furthermore, through UNCTAD facilitation, China has been providing valuable training in fishery resources management and development to the countries covered by the project. In 2016, China provided training for several participants at its Freshwater Fishery Research Centre. Currently, Portuguese-speaking countries, including Mozambique, are participating in an extensive training programme on the role of agriculture and fisheries in development in China.

Experience from China, Mauritius and Viet Nam has shown that there is an urgent need to identify a "regional centre of excellence". The objective of such a centre is to address persistent and emerging challenges facing the fishery sector in developing countries. This includes providing support to training of human resources and building institutional as well as regulatory capacities of developing countries.

Viet Nam is among the few developing countries that has transformed the fisheries sector to the industrial scale with aquaculture providing substantial impetus for such a transformation. The fishery sector in Viet Nam, directly or indirectly employs about 10 million people, 85 per cent of which is in aquaculture. The average annual export of fisheries (in value) in recent years from Viet Nam is in the range of US$10 billion in which the share of aquaculture is estimated at about 80 per cent. Such successful transformation of the fisheries sector can help other developing countries to draw practical and policy lessons in developing their respective fisheries sectors. As a concrete result of the project, the Asia Regional Centre of Excellence was established in the Nha Trang University of Viet Nam. A Memorandum of Understanding was signed between UNCTAD and the Nha Trang University in March 2018. The first taring course is scheduled to be delivered at the Regional Centre of Excellence from 29 October to 10 November 2018. UNCTAD, International Standards Organization, Marine Stewardship Council and possibly the Food and Agriculture Organization of the United Nations, together with Vietnamese professors and experts, will provide training courses at the Regional Centre of Excellence.

Mauritius was also identified as a possible regional centre of excellence, as the country has demonstrated considerable success in developing its fisheries sector. It has developed a well-functioning oceanographic institute, fishery research centre and full-fledged faculty. Mauritius also established regulatory and institutional capacity to comply with international food safety and quality standards and managed to attract investment to the sector. The combined role of these is to advance research and development in marine and aquaculture fishery and to harness the development potential of fisheries and the ocean economy. During an interregional training workshop, Mauritius expressed interest to become a regional centre of excellence and to serve as a hub for capacity-building in the fisheries and aquaculture sector for LDCs in the African and Asian regions. Mauritius will make available its expertise and institutional facilities. However, donor supports are needed to enable experts and technicians from LDCs and other vulnerable economies to learn from the experience of Mauritius. With donor support, selected

Many developing countries stand to benefit from this experience, in drawing lessons for their domestic fisheries sector.

practitioners from LDCs could benefit from a stand-alone hands-on training in developing the fisheries sector once or twice a year (either in Mauritius or in a selected LDC). Mauritius also stands ready to supply LDCs with fish feed and fish seed to strengthening domestic fisheries capacities.

Many LDCs and SIDS from Africa and Asia and the Pacific stand to benefit significantly from the experience of Mauritius in drawing lessons for their domestic fisheries sector. They also stand to gain from the relevant research capacities in the University of Mauritius, the Mauritius Oceanography Institute and the Fishery Research Centre of Mauritius, and from Nha Trang University of Viet Nam.

6.4 UNCTAD support on the African Continental Free Trade Area negotiations

The fragmentation of African small markets has hindered the continent from capitalizing on the economies of scale to trigger trade-led growth. Despite the 40 years of continental integration efforts, regional integration efforts were confined to subregional level and tariff and non-tariff protection have prevented the robust growth of trade within the continent. As a result, the share of intra-African trade has been low at around 10 per cent despite the recent rise due to low commodity prices. Boosting intra-African trade has come to be recognized as a priority for the content. Pan-African negotiations for an African Continental Free Trade Area were launched in June 2015, with the indicative target date for conclusion set for 2017, consistent with the African Union's Action Plan, "Boosting Intra-African Trade and the Establishment of a [Continental Free Trade Area]", as endorsed by the 18th African Union Summit of African Heads of States and Governments in January 2012.

The African Continental Free Trade Area negotiations are charged with several challenges intrinsic to the African context. These include its sheer size, many countries involved and heterogeneity among them, a multitude of subregional and inter-subregional integration processes, asymmetric level of integration achieved in different regional economic communities and the overlapping membership of several regional economic communities. These add to underlying economic constraints characterizing the continent, including low income levels and pervasive poverty, undiversified economies and high reliance on tariffs for fiscal revenue for many economies.

In order to facilitate pan-African continental integration efforts, UNCTAD has supported the African Union Commission and its members steadfastly and extensively. UNCTAD has supported African countries in conceptualizing the African economic continental integration to reform intra-African trade and economic integration for the economic transformation and development of Africa, and not limited to a trade agreement. UNCTAD has stood beside African countries prior to and since the Lagos Plan of Action, at the drafting of the Abuja Treaty and in the efforts to form the African Continental Free Trade Area since the formation of the African Union and the decision to create the African Continental Free Trade Area.

Using its extensive economic development experience in general and its expertise in Africa on trade negotiations and trade policies and on African integration and development, UNCTAD has supported the African Union and African countries in four main areas: (a) conceptualizing the African Continental Free Trade Area and developing different options in negotiating modalities in goods and services of the Area, and related issues including tariffs and non-tariff barriers; (b) assessing economic implications of different liberalization options to identify the best possible

> Using its expertise in economic development on trade negotiations and policies, and integration and development, UNCTAD has supported the African Union and African countries.

development options, such as in identifying priority products/services sectors or sensitive products, and assessing tariff liberalization modalities; (c) assisting them in finalizing the drafting of the African Continental Free Trade Area legal texts, including the framework agreement, as well as agreement on goods and services; and (d) assisting them in specific technical areas such as sanitary and phytosanitary measures, technical barriers to trade, non-tariff barriers to trade and dispute settlement, as well the phase II issue of competition policy. Thus, UNCTAD has participated and provided advice and technical support to the African Continental Free Trade Area Negotiating Forum, Technical Working Groups and Continental Task Force. UNCTAD have also assisted regional economic communities, such as ECOWAS and Tripartite Free Trade Area, in regional consultations and conducted training on formulation their regional positions on the African Continental Free Trade Area.

UNCTAD support contributed to the historic signature by leaders of 44 (out of 54) African States, in March 2018 in Kigali, of the agreement establishing the African Continental Free Trade Area and 47 of them signed the Kigali Declaration on creating the African Continental Free Trade Area. The African Continental Free Trade Area will cover goods and services and further aim at fostering cooperation in trade-related issues including competition policy, investment policy and intellectual property rights. The African Continental Free Trade Area will ultimately create a wider market of 55 African States comprising more than 1.2 billion people and $2.1 trillion combined national income, thus uniting markets, nations and peoples, and even consolidating existing regional economic communities into a single continental block. The Agreement is expected to increase intra-African trade and boost intra-African trade which presently hovers around 18 per cent of its total trade, create economies of scale for investment and RVCs, and foster a process of industrialization that is driven by internal demand. UNCTAD estimates suggests that the majority of African countries will gain from the Continental Free Trade Area with the average welfare gains projected at about 1 per cent of GDP.

In light of its long-standing support and contribution, UNCTAD today is recognized by the African Union Commission as a legitimate strategic partner alongside the Economic Commission for Africa and African Development Bank. The African Union Commission, member States and regional economic communities have expressed appreciation for UNCTAD contributions, including publicly, as, for instance, the Chair of the African Union Commission did at the 30th ordinary session of the African Union Assembly of Heads of State and Government session in January 2018.

6.5 From raw materials to exporting finished leather products

Africa has doubled its growth rate in the 2000s as compared to 1990s, though growth has not been transformative. In fact, the contribution of the manufacturing sector in total value added has been steadily declining in many of the region's countries, indicating de-industrialization. One of the most important challenges facing African countries is triggering structural transformation and, in the process, creating more value addition in their exports and generating higher employment. The leather and leather products industry provides a tremendous opportunity to the region to form RVCs and add greater value to the region's exports as well as play a transformative role. At present, the region is the largest source of the basic raw material of the industry, i.e. leather, but exports it with little value addition.

Furthermore, the region's global imports of leather products have been steadily rising since the past two decades. Given the labour-intensive nature of the industry, it can also generate large-scale employment for low-skilled labour.

Over the years, the global leather industry has become highly fragmented and production has spread across different continents, with raw hides and skins, part processed leather, finished leather, leather components and leather products being widely imported and exported. One of the main reasons for this fragmentation has been shifting out of processing of leather from developed countries into least developed and developing countries. The increasing cost of labour and stringent laws relating to environmental pollution in the developed world have been mainly responsible for the shift. Ample availability of raw hides and skins in developing countries has further encouraged emergence of GVCs in the industry. It has been argued that Africa could gain tremendously by forming its own RVCs, rather than linking into GVCs.

In this context, in collaboration with the African Expert–Import Bank and Commonwealth Secretariat, UNCTAD undertook a project on identifying potential RVCs in leather and leather products in Africa, which was successfully completed in 2017. The project produced a technical study which applied rigorous methodology to identify potential RVCs that could be formed within Africa in leather and leather products. The study found that three subregions cover around 98 per cent of trade in leather and leather products in Africa. These are COMESA, ECOWAS and the Southern African Customs Union. These three regional trade blocs, comprising 40 countries, together contribute around 98 per cent of exports and 99 per cent of imports of leather and leather products.

The study generated three lists for each of the 40 countries, indicating the ways in which a country could link into the RVC in leather and leather products:

- List of outputs or finished leather products, where the country has potential to export to the regional and global markets.

- List of inputs, i.e. primary and processed leather including other identified inputs (for example, chemicals used for dyes), which can be sourced by a country from the region at a lower cost, as compared to what it is currently importing from outside the region, though the region has the supply capacity.

- List of leather and leather products where the country needs FDIs to engage in the RVC for the leather industry.

Country- and regional-level policy suggestions were made on promoting and initiating RVCs. Furthermore, policies were suggested on promoting intraregional FDIs in leather industry.

The findings of the study were discussed with the industry at three regional stakeholders' consultations organized in collaboration with the Africa Leather and Leather Product Institute. One of the important limitations identified by the study on forming RVCs and successfully exporting finished leather products was low design capacity in Africa. The designs did not "speak" to world markets. In order to overcome this limitation, the Commonwealth Secretariat, with the support of UNCTAD and the Africa Leather and Leather Product Institute, launched the Regional Design Studio in Ethiopia in May 2016, where the African designers could be trained by world class designers. The first designers' training workshop brought together more than 50 designers in the leather sector from 11 Eastern and Southern Africa countries, namely Burundi, Eritrea, Ethiopia, Eswatini, Kenya, Malawi, Rwanda, Sudan, Uganda, Zambia and Zimbabwe, and a leading design firm from Canada provided the training.

> The study generated three lists each for 40 countries, indicating the ways in which to link into the regional value chain.

The regional design studio is expected to provide continuous support to the enterprises in Africa for using design strategically in a fast-changing business landscape. The studio will boost design capacity in exports of leather products at the regional and global levels making RVCs most cost competitive and successful globally.

The regional design studio[28] is now in the process of establishing memorandums of understanding with premier design institutions in China, India, Italy, the Republic of Korea and Turkey.

6.6 Capacity-building to reform international investment agreements

Developing countries face a number of international investment agreement regime-related challenges that include dealing with broadly drafted provisions focusing almost exclusively on investment protection, the absence of provisions on the right to regulate of host States, on sustainable development objectives and ensuring responsible investment. These challenges are in addition to the need to manage an increasing number of investor–State dispute settlement cases that have not only heightened the profile of international investment agreements, but also highlighted their unanticipated – and partially undesired – side effects.

Since 2012, UNCTAD has worked to improve the capacity of international investment agreement negotiators from developing countries, based on its *Investment Policy Framework for Sustainable Development*, to formulate international investment rules that effectively foster sustainable development, safeguards the right to regulate and responsible investment. Through its technical assistance work, UNCTAD has delivered regional trainings, seminars and workshops and offered ad hoc advice to strengthen the capacity of beneficiary countries in handling the complexities of the international investment agreement regime and to better manage and prevent investor–State dispute settlement cases.

One example of a successful South–South capacity-building model is the annual UNCTAD–Islamic Development Bank workshop on issues related to international investment agreements. Since 2012, the workshops have trained over 360 government officials from over 45 developing countries on issues related to international investment agreements and investor–State dispute settlement. They follow a thematic agenda dealing with the most pressing issues arising from international investment agreements. These range from ensuring policy coherence between international investment agreements, national regulation and development strategies; managing investor-State disputes; designing clear and explicit international investment agreement clauses; balancing investors' rights and obligations (in line with corporate social responsibility principles); safeguarding policy space for other public policies (e.g. climate change, labour, health); and negotiating strategies.

The workshops have encouraged stakeholders from a broad spectrum of the investment community to address challenges, harness opportunities and develop policy solutions for creating synergy between investment policies and sustainable development goals. In implementing the workshops, UNCTAD and the Islamic Development Bank partnered with several regional and international organizations, the private sector and academia.

The workshops tangible impact can be demonstrated as beneficiary countries formulate a new generation of sustainable development-oriented international investment agreements. For example, many negotiators of new-generation

Since 2012, UNCTAD has worked to improve the capacity of international investment agreement negotiators from developing countries.

[28] http://comsecllpidesignstudio.allpi.int/index.php/news-updates.

international investment agreements have attended and benefited from UNCTAD capacity-building programmes and regional workshops before concluding treaties that reflect a balance between State commitments and investor obligations and that address sustainable development imperatives. Other beneficiary countries have reviewed their treaty networks and revised their treaty models in line with the UNCTAD reform package for the international investment regime (2017d).

Other noticeable impacts relate to the enhanced awareness of developing countries policymakers and negotiators on the seriousness of the commitments included in international investment agreements and their implications on developing countries' right to regulate investment in their territories. International investment agreement negotiators from developing countries are now more cautious and engage in lengthy negotiations with third parties as opposed to expeditious conclusions of broadly drafted international investment agreements in the 1980s and 1990s.

At the regional level, the impact of UNCTAD capacity-building activities has been noticeable, particularly when looking at the content of new regional South–South investment agreements and instruments that as discussed above, include many of the recommendations found in the UNCTAD *Investment Policy Framework for Sustainable Development* (2015c), UNCTAD road map for international investment agreement reform (2015b) and UNCTAD reform package for the international investment regime (2017d).

CHAPTER 7

South–South cooperation in times of "Industry 4.0"

7.1 Digital industrialization for achieving the 2030 Agenda

The world economy is increasingly affected by digital technologies, potentially disrupting industrial organization, skills development, production and trade.[29] The key technologies driving the evolving digital economy include: (a) advanced robotics, (b) artificial intelligence, (c) "Internet of things", (d) cloud computing; (e) big data analytics, (f) three-dimensional printing and (g) digital payment systems (UNCTAD, 2017f).

The rapidly growing presence of these technologies in industrial production has resulted in the major upheaval in modern manufacturing labelled "Industry 4.0". But the rapid evolution and uptake of digital technologies can also be seen across services of various kinds, including transport, communications and infrastructure. Therefore, they also play an increasingly important role in social and political life, research, services, transportation and agriculture.

Increased digitalization of economic activities and transactions creates new opportunities and challenges for trade and development. It can help smaller businesses and entrepreneurs in developing countries to connect with global markets more easily and open new ways of generating income. ICTs, e-commerce and other digital applications can be leveraged to promote entrepreneurship, including the empowerment of women as entrepreneurs and traders, and to support productive activities, decent job creation, creativity and innovation. Furthermore, mobile and digital solutions are contributing to facilitating greater financial inclusion. Small firms in developing countries with sufficient connectivity may be able to access various cloud services and make use of crowdfunding through online platforms. However, the extent to which countries, in particular developing economies, can seize these opportunities varies considerably. Most developing countries, particularly the least developed and small island countries, lack digital capacities. These countries face the challenge of being left behind if they do not develop digitally, especially in the context of a growing digital divide.

> **Box 7**
> **Online platforms and the trading market place**
>
> Various forms of digital platforms play a central role in the evolving landscape for e-commerce and the digital economy. By reducing transaction and search costs, as well as frictions, digital platforms enable those offering assets or services to connect more easily with those wishing to consume them, creating opportunities for new types of trade.
>
> Benefiting from economies of scale and network effects, a few major global online marketplaces have captured significant parts of the overall market. Nevertheless, a growing number of digital platforms have emerged in developing countries
>
> Digital platforms lead to efficiency gains derived from lower transaction costs and information asymmetries supported by rating systems, lower consumer prices, increased access to markets, more competition, better use of underutilized resources and flexibility for providers of services.
>
> Net benefits from online platforms can, however, be unevenly distributed. Moreover, there are concerns that the market power of certain platforms may lead to abuse of dominant positions, anti-competitive practices, data protection and privacy issues, tax erosion and negative effects on jobs. The lower cost of consumption may increase the volume of resources used and carbon emissions.
>
> *Source*: UNCTAD, 2018d; UNCTAD, 2017f.

[29] For more information, see UNCTAD flagships reports, such as the *Information Economy Report, Trade and Development Report, Technology* and *Innovation Report* and *World Investment Report*.

7.2 Challenges of "Industry 4.0" for the global South

Development gains from digitalization are not automatic, and there are significant challenges associated with the evolution of digitalization. There is a risk that digitalization will lead to increased polarization and widening income inequalities, as productivity gains may accrue mainly to a few, already wealthy and skilled individuals, as well as to the enterprises that are already most prepared. Various digital divides in both access and use of ICT are prevalent, notably between rich and poor, across and within countries (UNCTAD, 2017f).

The advent of Industry 4.0 has led to a rapid rise in the digital content of industrial production, blurring the boundaries between products and services. Digital industrialization is impacting all stages of production. Higher use of digital services and digital technologies at the production stage, as well as at pre- and post-production stages, via big-data analytics, artificial intelligence and e-commerce can provide important opportunities to developing countries to upgrade in GVCs and benefit from increased employment opportunities. It has been estimated that, within the next decade, the digital economy will account for almost 25 per cent of global GDP. However, if developing countries are not digitally prepared, the existing digital divide could deepen, leading to a deepening of the "smile curve" depicting the value captured by different production stages in GVCs (UNCTAD, 2018a), which is mainly concentrated in pre- and post-production stages of GVCs. This can in turn lead to further downgrading of the value attributed to the manufacturing stage, where most developing countries are stuck.

To boost industrialization, there is a need to develop capacities for using big data analytics, the "Internet of things", robotics, artificial intelligence and other digital technologies. Along with physical infrastructure, developing countries will need to develop their digital infrastructure, which includes ICT infrastructure, cloud-computing infrastructure and data infrastructure, along with associated digital skills.[30] However, it is extremely challenging for most developing countries to leapfrog into digital economies without supporting policies at the national and regional levels. In this context, regional digital cooperation can help developing countries in advancing in their efforts to industrialize.

On their own, developing countries may not be able to digitally industrialize, i.e. increase digital content in their industrial production through increased use of digital technologies and digital services. Many developing countries, especially the LDCs, may not be adequately prepared to capture the many opportunities emerging from digitalization and, particularly, to take advantage of technology for productive and innovative activities. Major shortcomings relate to the skills needed to harness digital tools, legal and regulatory frameworks, and access to financing of entrepreneurship and innovation.[31] The lack of official statistics in developing countries represents another serious disadvantage for policymakers in these countries as it hampers their ability to design and monitor evidence-based policymaking.

To succeed in the digital economy, and to benefit from "Industry 4.0", a broad approach is needed to build capabilities to take advantage of technologies for productive and innovative activities. There is a wide spectrum of policy areas that should be addressed in a holistic manner, such as digital infrastructure, education and skills development, the labour market, competition, science, technology and innovation and fiscal issues, as well as trade and industrial policies (see also UNCTAD, 2018d).

> **Development gains from digitalization are not automatic, and there are significant challenges associated with the evolution of digitalization.**

> **Regional digital cooperation can help developing countries in advancing in their efforts to industrialize.**

[30] See United Nations, 2018, on building digital competencies to benefit from existing and emerging technologies, with a special focus on gender and youth dimensions, and https://unctad.org/en/pages/newsdetails. aspx?OriginalVersionID=1756.

[31] See http://unctad.org/en/ Pages/Publications/E-Trade-Readiness-Assessment.aspx.

7.3 UNCTAD agenda for South–South cooperation and "Industry 4.0"

South–South cooperation, in the form of "regional digital cooperation" between member countries within the region is essential for digital industrialization of the South. Regional digital cooperation can be an additional element in the ongoing regional integration processes in the South. UNCTAD (2018e) has proposed a 10-point progressive digital cooperation agenda for industrialization, which includes building a data economy; building cloud computing facilities; strengthening broadband infrastructure; promoting e-commerce in the region; promoting regional digital payments; progressing on a single digital market in the region;[32] sharing experiences on e-government; forging partnerships for building smart cities; promoting digital innovations and technologies; and building statistics for measuring digitization. The key components of such a digital cooperation agenda are as follows:

a. South–South digital cooperation for building a data economy

in the digital economy, data are the raw material which gets transformed into digital intelligence. Processing and analysis of big amounts of data have evolved very rapidly in recent years thanks to technological progress and digitalization. Under new business models that have emerged, including digital platforms, global companies can extract data, which individually may be of limited value, and create value by aggregating and analysing the data. This value resulting from the conversion of data into digital intelligence can then be monetized. Owning this digital intelligence implies a key asset for controlling large parts of the value in the digital economy. This intelligence risks concentrating in the developed economies and with a few big tech firms, contributing to growing digital monopolies.[33] Of the top 25 big tech firms (in terms of market capitalization), 14 are based in the United States of America, 3 in the European Union, 3 in China, 4 in other Asian countries and 1 in Africa. The top three big technology firms in the United States have an average market capitalization of more than $400 billion, compared with an average of $200 billion in the top big tech firms in China, $123 billion in Asia, $69 billion in Europe and $66 billion in Africa (see also UNCTAD, 2018a).

South–South digital cooperation can help build data economies in the developing countries. For building a data economy, countries in the South first need to define policies with respect to ownership of data. Special attention should be given to issues related to data ownership, collection and analysis, as well as data privacy and protection.[34] The need to regulate or implement policies to tackle risks, should be adapted depending on the nature of data. In most countries, data are owned by those who collect or store data. There are no national laws preventing a domestic or foreign firm from taking, using or abusing a country's data or the data produced by its citizens.

Protecting and regulating data flows by Governments may allow them to share regionally. Given the economies of scale, regional pool of data would allow building of digital infrastructure within the region more cost effectively (UNCTAD, 2018a). But there is a need to have a clear distinction between personal and non-personal data. Although non-personal data needs to be allowed to flow freely within the region, ensuring protection of personal data is extremely important, especially in building trust within a region.

Since there are different types of data (public, open, personal and commercial data), their impact on the economy and society may vary. Since the digital intelligence

[32] See, for example, the European Union's single digital market initiatives.

[33] See UNCTAD (2018a), chapter 2, on the concentration of digital platforms mainly in advanced countries, and studies such as Foster and McChesney (2011) and Van Alstyne et al. (2016).

[34] See UNCTAD (2016f). Issues of data protection regulations and international data flows and implications for trade and development will also feature at the third session of the UNCTAD Intergovernmental Group of Experts on E-commerce and the Digital Economy in 2019.

capacity in developing countries is limited, they are constrained in their potential to capture the economic value of data. South–South cooperation can play an important role in fostering improved capacity in developing countries to monetize data and to develop relevant policies and regulations. A well-defined framework for data collection, storage, elaboration and flows will enable the emergence of value generation activities around data, and appropriation of that value by players from the South.

b. South–South cooperation for building cloud computing facilities

Cloud computing facilities at the regional level, by providing easy remote access to computing services in all the countries within the region, can provide significant benefits in terms of cost, flexibility, efficiency and scalability. South–South cooperation for developing "regional clouds" can greatly benefit the countries in sharing experiences and developing advanced digital skills. As global production processes move from "mass production" to "customized production", defined data governance policies and regulatory frameworks may provide countries and a given region a comparative advantage in, for example, customizing three-dimensionally printed manufactured products. Big data analytical skills can be developed through regional support, which can benefit all citizens and local enterprises within a region and boost intraregional trade and investments.[35]

c. South–South cooperation for strengthening broadband infrastructure

High-speed broadband access to increases powerful computing and storage capacity, and drastically reduces costs of ICT equipment and data management. It has facilitated the process of digitalization. Broadband access and use are critical enablers of the digital economy (UNCTAD, 2017f). Despite increased connectivity, broadband use is still very limited in LDCs, where it remains unaffordable for most people. Fixed broadband prices can be three times higher in developing countries than in developed countries, and mobile broadband twice as high (International Telecommunication Union, 2018). LDCs rely almost entirely on mobile broadband networks.

Improving the quality and affordability of broadband is essential to enable additional investments in and use of data centres, cloud computing, big data and Internet of things (Global Connectivity Index, 2017). Increased availability and use of broadband services can help to improve social inclusion and productivity in the South (Mack and Faggian, 2013). Providing support at the regional level to build national broadband infrastructure can help in boosting the regional competitiveness. South–South cooperation and triangular cooperation can play an important role in this regard. Some of the developing countries such as Brazil and China have signed agreements with the European Union to develop 5G mobile technology. These countries, as well as India can provide a key support to other developing countries through investing in development of their broadband infrastructure.

d. South–South cooperation for promoting e-commerce in a region

Regional data economy and regional digital infrastructure, especially cloud computing and broadband infrastructures will enhance regional e-commerce and enable producers and suppliers to have easy, affordable and fast access to the regional markets, boosting regional integration. However, this will require regional

[35] See also UNCTAD, 2018a, and UNCTAD, 2017f. In addition, the European Cloud Initiative for which documentation suggests that the Initiative will strengthen Europe's position in data-driven innovation, improve competitiveness and cohesion, and help create a digital single market in Europe (see https://ec.europa.eu/digital-single-market/en/%20european-cloud-initiative and https://ec.europa.eu/digital-single-market/en/%20european-cloud-initiative). See also the Middle East North Africa Cloud Alliance's Cloud Competitiveness Index 2017, launched for the countries of the Gulf Cooperation Council (https://www.menacloud.org/Doc/MENACA%20 CCI%20(c).pdf) and the Digital Agenda for Latin America and the Caribbean (https://conferenciaelac.cepal.org/6/sites/elac2020/files/cmsi.6_agenda_digital.pdf).

e-commerce strategy which in turn should support national e-commerce policies. National e-commerce policies should aim at developing the national e-commerce platforms and putting in place rules and regulations governing e-commerce. UNCTAD supports countries seeking to formulate a national e-commerce strategy through effective diagnostics, policy advice and customized strategy development.[36] A regional approach to develop e-commerce strategies should seek to ensure that national rules and regulations on e-commerce are harmonized or compatible. Regional cooperation needs to focus on cross border contract rules and regulations for consumer protection; data protection; digital payment infrastructure[37] within a region; reducing cost of parcel delivery; and addressing issues related to geo-blocking and cybersecurity.

Regional digital cooperation can further strengthen the global cost-competitiveness of RVCs. It could also consider issues related to competition policy implications of international e-commerce platforms and ways to facilitate the growth of national and regional e-commerce platforms in the market. Moreover, regional and international policy frameworks should allow countries the necessary policy space for properly capturing value for development from e-commerce.

e. South–South cooperation on digital payments

digital payments are an essential requirement for the development of a digital economy. For African countries, the role of mobile money is particularly relevant in this context. In a CIGI–IPSOS–UNCTAD global survey of Internet users, 79 per cent of the Kenyan respondents expressed mobile payment as their preferred method of paying for goods and services purchased online. However, for developing countries advancing from cash to cashless payments is extremely challenging and will require developing well-regulated financial sector which includes commercial banks, financial institutions and other e-money institutions with appropriate rules around consumer data protection. This makes regional cooperation in digital payments challenging, but there exist some best practices in the South. SADC members have developed an Integrated Regional Electronic Settlement System at the regional level, which includes national and regional clearing houses to facilitate payments between financial institutions.

f. Progressing on regional single digital markets

A regional digital single market has to be seen as the ultimate goal for digital integration within the regional blocs of the South. This would imply seamless access to online activities by all consumers and producers in the region, irrespective of their nationality and country of residence. However, this goal may be extremely difficult to achieve with the existing digital capacities in the regional blocs of the South. Rich learnings are provided by the European Union's policy on a digital single market strategy, which was adopted in 2015. This has 16 initiatives and aims at maximizing growth potential of the digital economy. However, this may not be immediately replicable by the South.

g. South–South sharing of experiences on e-government

South–South sharing experiences on e-government[38] is important for building adequate policies in support of all productive sectors. "Ease of doing business" has a particular positive impact in the manufacturing sector. South–South cooperation agenda can greatly benefit from sharing of experiences on e-government, which has been successfully implemented by some of the developing countries. The sharing

---

[36] See http://unctad.org/en/Pages/DTL/ STI_and_ICTs/ICT4D-Policies.aspx.

[37] See for example the SADC Integrated Regional Electronic Settlement System. See also Glenbrook and Southern African Development Community Banking Association, 2017.

[38] E-government refers to the use of information technologies by government agencies to deliver services to citizens (G2C), business enterprises (G2B), government employees (G2E) and other government agencies (G2G).

of experiences will also help in identifying most cost-effective practices and avoid wastage of limited public resources. Some of the developing countries, like India, can share its experience of launching initiatives under the National E-Governance Plan. This is a progressive plan of India which promotes e-governance in a holistic manner. Similarly, China has rich experiences to share in this area.

h. Forging South–South partnerships for building smart sustainable cities

The application of major "Industry 4.0" technologies is vital in making cities smart and sustainable in line with Sustainable Development Goal 11. Technologies such as artificial intelligence applied to smart grids, renewable energy, waste and water management may contribute to energy efficiency, water and food security, and effectively address climate change and environmental issues.[39] Similarly, "Industry 4.0" technologies, including sensors and inter connected physical devices, may contribute to developing Smart sustainable cities where key public services like urban transportation health care, education and security are more efficiently provided.[40] Smart sustainable cities can also help in overcoming the limitations of traditional urban development by using key "Industry 4.0" technologies and sound infrastructure. While a number of countries in the North are progressively building their smart sustainable cities, very few developing countries have been successful in this area. South–South cooperation can help developing countries progress fast on building smart sustainable cities, which can help save financial resources in the future due to high returns to investments. Sharing knowledge and innovations with developing countries can lead to technology transfers and spill overs giving the needed boost to the digital industrialization process in developing countries.

i. South–South cooperation on promoting digital innovations and technologies

Innovations are at the heart of "Industry 4.0". Many developing countries are in a process of incentivizing digital start-ups to encourage digital innovations. This is an area where South–South cooperation can greatly contribute by pooling human and financial resources to stimulate and share innovative ideas and develop digital technologies. There is a need for the development banks, such as the BRICS bank – the New Development Bank, Asian Development Bank and African Development Banks, to financially support innovations and start-ups in the South. South–South investments in digital technologies can foster technology transfers and innovations, if they allow source-code sharing and encourage tailoring of the digital technologies from open source codes to their needs and requirements. Technology cooperation at the regional level can greatly benefit the South.

j. South–South cooperation for building statistics for measuring digitalization

The contribution of digitization is difficult to measure and compare across developing countries due to lack of statistics. Digital technologies lead to increase in manufacturing productivity both directly (through digitalization of manufacturing products, e.g. three-dimensional printing) as well as indirectly (through developing software using artificial intelligence), however statistical tools are still unable to capture these contributions. Developing countries urgently need to develop statistical tools to capture the extent and progress towards digitalization. The European Union's initiative of constructing a composite digital economy and society

---

[39] See, for example, the Buenos Aires Declaration of 30 May 2018 (International Telecommunication Union, 2018).

[40] Trends and challenges in the development of smart cities are discussed in the report of the Secretary-General to the 19th session of the CSTD. https://unctad.org/meetings/en/SessionalDocuments/ecn162016d2_en.pdf

index (for European countries can be a reference for developing countries in which data and information can be collected accordingly. In addition, the UNCTAD B2C eCommerce Index, which covers 144 countries, provides some useful guidance in this respect, but developing countries should also begin collecting and publishing their own data in this important area. South–South and triangular cooperation can lead the way for developing countries to develop statistical tools and capture the required data and information. These topics will be covered in intergovernmental discussed in a newly created Working Group on Measuring E-commerce and the Digital Economy, under the UNCTAD Intergovernmental Group of Experts E-commerce and the Digital Economy. The Working Group, which will convene in the third quarter of 2019, can be of use to developing countries to share experiences, discuss priorities and needs for capacity-building.

7.4 UNCTAD framework on South–South cooperation for technology and innovation

South–South collaboration may enable developing countries to tailor their partnerships in ways that address those priorities and serve broader and economic goals. South partner countries may have a better understanding on the ways and means of overcoming innovation constraints facing other developing countries and they may have more cost and context-effective technologies. To exploit these advantages, UNCTAD proposes a framework to guide South–South cooperation on technology and innovation (see table). In addition, box 8 list some of UNCTAD South–South cooperation initiatives/forums in the areas of science, technology and innovation, and the digital economy.

Some proposed features and principles for South–South cooperation

Interactions promoted for specific areas	• Exchange of innovation policy experiences and policy frameworks for technology and innovation. • Technology exchange and flows aimed at increasing technology absorptive capacities in the private and public sectors • Transfer of technologies in key sectors of importance for public wellbeing.
Principles to follow	• Prioritize technological needs of developing countries and LDCs • Aim at sharing and better integrating the lessons learned from the on-going catch up experiences of other developing countries in building innovation capabilities through proactive policies • Promote important means of technological learning, particularly through alliances and technology transfer initiatives • Make South–South FDI more technology oriented • Pool developing-country resources to address common technological challenges

Source: UNCTAD, 2012b.

Box 8

South–South cooperation for science, technology, innovation and the digital economy

United Nations Commission on Science and Technology for Development. A forum where States and other stakeholders can come together to: (a) assess what the future could bring; (b) engage in technological foresight from a development perspective and (c) develop consensus on how a collective future can be shaped through deeper common understanding of national and international actions to maximize the development impact of technology and innovation, including with regard to digitalization. The Commission on Science and Technology for Development has, over the years, incubated several important initiatives which promote South–South cooperation and capacity-building in science, technology and innovation, such as the Network of Centres of Excellence. The Commission on Science and Technology for Development has also provided the platform to facilitate capacity-building activities in collaboration between China and other developing countries.

The eTrade for all initiative.[a] Provides a platform for enhancing the transparency and effectiveness in the provision of technical assistance that can help developing countries strengthen their readiness to engage in ecommerce and the digital economy. This initiative can be used to identify needs and matching resources to support South–South collaboration in the area of e-commerce and the digital economy.

Some ongoing initiatives. Aimed at building the readiness of countries in understanding and managing policy in the area of e-commerce and the digital economy:

- Technical assistance to support regional groupings on e-commerce and related law reform (EAC, ECOWAS, ASEAN, Latin American Economic System, Latin American Integration Association and the Caribbean Community).

- Assessments of the enabling environment for e-commerce in LDCs (UNCTAD rapid e-Trade readiness assessments), which shed light on obstacles faced to reap the benefits of e-commerce.

- Partnerships with regional organizations including regional development banks, regional commissions, civil society organizations and the private sector, including by leveraging the UNCTAD-led eTrade for all initiative.

A first ever Africa E-commerce Week will be organized in Nairobi, on 10–14 December 2018. Such regional meetings can help foster South–South discussion and collaboration in key areas.

Source: UNCTAD.
[a] etradeforall.org.

ANNEX

South–South Cooperation for Implementation of the 2030 Agenda for Sustainable Development: A Trade and Development Perspective

Preparatory thematic consultation towards the Second High-level United Nations Conference on South–South Cooperation

Geneva, 5 November 2018

Organized by the United Nations Conference on Trade and Development (UNCTAD) in cooperation with the Permanent Mission of the Argentine Republic to the United Nations Office and other international organizations in Geneva.

Summary and non-binding recommendations

A. Introduction

1. As part of the preparatory processes for the Second High-level United Nations Conference on South–South Cooperation (BAPA+40 Conference), the United Nations Office for South–South Cooperation invited Member States, United Nations agencies, intergovernmental and non-governmental organizations, international financial institutions, think tanks, academic institutions, the private sector, the scientific community and philanthropic organizations to convene, contribute to and participate in the preparatory processes for the 2019 Conference, providing valuable inputs that will inform deliberations of Member States towards the adoption of an outcome document.

2. UNCTAD prepared a draft version of the present report to provide background for an informal thematic consultation, held in advance of the BAPA+40 Conference on 5 November 2018. The thematic consultation's overarching theme was "South–South Cooperation for Implementation of the 2030 Agenda for Sustainable Development: A Trade and Development Perspective".

3. The informal thematic consultation covered South–South trade, investment and financing, South–South technology transfers and partnerships for technological innovation and South–South cooperation and "Industry 4.0", over the course of three sessions. A summary of key points made during discussions at the three sessions (section B) and non-binding recommendations (section C) are presented below.

B. Informal thematic consultation: Summary*

4. The United Nations Conference on Trade and Development (UNCTAD), in cooperation with the Permanent Mission of the Argentine Republic to the United Nations Office and other international organizations in Geneva, organized an informal thematic consultation on 5 November 2018. The consultation's overarching theme was "South–South Cooperation for Implementation of the 2030 Agenda for Sustainable Development: A Trade and Development Perspective". The consultation brought together more than 80 participants, including 43 representatives from member States of UNCTAD, 2 representatives from intergovernmental organizations, 9 representatives from United Nations bodies and specialized agencies, 6 representatives from non-governmental organizations and academia, as well as staff of the UNCTAD secretariat. Participants discussed and shared experiences in South–South cooperation over three sessions, namely on (a) South–South trade, investment and financing (b) South–South cooperation for technology transfers and partnerships for technological innovation; and (c) South–South cooperation and "Industry 4.0".

5. The remainder of this summary includes key points made during the discussions, followed by non-binding recommendations proposed during the informal thematic consultation. It is the intention of UNCTAD that this summary

* The views expressed in this summary do not necessarily reflect the views of the United Nations or its officials or Member States.

and its non-binding recommendations will inform and contribute to Member States' negotiations on a forward-looking outcome document, to be adopted by the BAPA+40 Conference in Buenos Aires in 2019.

Welcoming and opening remarks and presentation of the UNCTAD background document

6. The Deputy Secretary-General of UNCTAD welcomed participants and stated that the BAPA+40 Conference would be an opportunity to reflect on the 40 years that had passed since the adoption of the Buenos Aires Plan of Action for Promoting and Implementing Technical Cooperation among Developing Countries in 1978. She added that UNCTAD dedicated a very significant part of its work programme to promoting and implementing South–South cooperation.

7. The Permanent Representative of Argentina in Geneva recalled that, 40 years earlier, delegations from 138 countries gathered in Argentina to adopt the Buenos Aires Plan of Action for Promoting and Implementing Technical Cooperation among Developing Countries, also known as BAPA. He pointed out that the March 2019 conference in Argentina would be a unique opportunity for reviewing trends in South–South cooperation and progress made by the international community, in particular the United Nations, in supporting and promoting such cooperation and in identifying challenges and suggestions to overcome those challenges. He noted that Argentina actively supported and promoted South–South cooperation and triangular cooperation, as a main platform to deliver on international cooperation. Argentina participated in different regional and international initiatives, encouraging the creation of partnerships and sharing experiences in different domains of public policies for the purpose of ensuring social inclusion and sustainable development at the national, regional and global levels. The country's experience in the field of South–South and triangular cooperation had proven that, through dialogue and the search for complementarity, it is possible to achieve results with social, economic and environmental impact that led to well-being and progress in our societies. He hoped that the conclusions drawn from the thematic consultation in the lead up to BAPA+40 Conference resulted in valuable recommendations that looked innovatively at the issues at the heart of the matter and made specific suggestions that countries could consider, whether the aim was to prepare strategies or to take effective actions to achieve the Sustainable Development Goals under the 2030 Agenda for Sustainable Development.

8. The Deputy Secretary-General of UNCTAD, in presenting the draft background report entitled "Forging a path beyond border: the global South", noted that it drew on the collective experience of UNCTAD in support of South–South cooperation and in pursuit of the Sustainable Development Goals. The report documented how, over the past 40 years, there had been steep intensification of South–South cooperation, with developing countries emerging as regional and global players in almost every region. The report finds that though the so-called "rise of the South" had prompted enthusiasm, it had also remained largely uneven and incomplete. The idea of developing countries as engines of the global economy remained unrealized for the most part. The widespread shift towards convergence of developing countries, observed in the first decade of the 2000s, was short-lived, due largely to a super cycle commodity boom driven primarily by China. After the global financial crisis, the boom had receded, with commodity prices falling, and had not been sustained in the decade since the crisis.

9. The Deputy Secretary-General highlighted some of the observations put forward by the report:

   a. Developing countries should double down on their regional economic cooperation on trade, finance, investment and technology. Regional value chains and regional financing solutions were not only a promising way forward for Sustainable Development Goal achievement, but also for countering rising trade tensions and the backlash against globalization, as currently seen at the global level.

   b. Developing countries should assess their participation in South–South cooperation by the degree to which it built productive capacity and helps structural transformation. South–South partnerships must avoid replicating the uneven relationships that had sometimes characterized North–South cooperation

   c. Developing countries should work together to meet the challenges of the new digital era. The growing digital divide was probably one of the biggest emerging trade and development challenges that developing countries would face over the medium term. Developing countries needed to build their collective capacity to overcome those challenges and not make the same mistakes with digitalization that many had made with globalization.

Session I: South–South trade, investment and financing

10. South–South cooperation had the potential to become the new engine of growth for developing countries and could help them achieve the objectives of the 2030 Agenda. South–South cooperation provided additional opportunities for developing countries to increase trade and investment and access finance and technology.

11. Despite the rise of South–South cooperation in the areas of trade, investment and finance over the past four decades, there was a long way to go to fully take advantage of the potential of South–South cooperation for achieving the 2030 Agenda for Sustainable Development.

12. South–South trade had expanded rapidly over the past decades and its share in developing countries' total exports increased significantly. For example, in 2016, one quarter (25 per cent) of world total trade was conducted among developing countries. However, the aggregate figures masked important regional imbalances and diversity, as Africa and Latin America, for instance, were yet to fully exploit South–South trade. Trade with some emerging developing countries represented a high proportion of South–South trade. One example mentioned was the fact that total exports between South America and Africa amounted to US$15.475 million and total imports between South America and Africa amounted to US$7,452 million. Concerns were expressed that Africa and Latin America, though sharing many similarities, had limited trading linkages (low trade flows) and, for instance, few direct flights between the regions.

13. Latin America and Africa had significant potential to increase their trade and investments. The full potential of South–South trade was therefore yet to be realized and much needed to be done. Better connectivity between the two regions could contribute significantly to South–South volumes of trade and investments.

14. In the last few years, many developing countries had intensified their efforts to promote South–South regional integration, with the formation of the African Continental Free Trade Area a notable example. Regional South–South trade integration and cooperation, particularly when supported by regional investment and financial cooperation, could contribute to boosting intraregional trade.

15. Regional value chains in the South could provide an alternate solution to ongoing challenges in the global trade scenario and also help in building productive capacity in developing countries and diversifying production and export structures.

16. South–South trade cooperation at the interregional level, especially the Global System of Trade Preferences among Developing Countries, could play an important role as a viable platform for South–South trade cooperation. Completing ongoing domestic ratification of the São Paulo round results remained of critical importance as its entry into force would showcase the Global System of Trade Preferences and potentially trigger broader support for its revitalization. UNCTAD should play a central role in supporting members of the Global System of Trade Preferences in the endeavour, including by measuring, assessing and estimating South–South trade and gains from the Global System of Trade Preferences. BAPA+40 provided an excellent opportunity for raising the profile of the Global System of Trade Preferences and mobilizing broad-based support for the South–South trade mechanism.

17. South–South cooperation had not realized it full potential. Limited institutional capacity, the priority of South–South issues on national agendas and politics had been the main challenges. To realize South–South potential in different domains, there was a need to address limited capacity through technical cooperation and to increase dialogues involving wider multi-stakeholders, including promotion of South–South cooperation.

18. 18. China had contributed significantly to South–South trade and investments and was an important contributor to growth in the South. Important lessons from the success story of China needed to be shared with and within the South.

19. Financial and monetary cooperation was of great importance to the South and could contribute to its development objectives. It could also help strengthen the international financial architecture by providing means for developing countries to participate more equitably and on a basis of solidarity.

20. South–South institutions and mechanisms were already helping defend developing countries against crises of balance of payments and foreign liquidity shortage. Regional reserve funds and bilateral swaps worth trillions of dollars were responding to crises and building resilience. They offered the urgent financial support needed, quickly and without policy conditionality. However, South–South cooperation in that regard was still incomplete and uneven. It needed to be strengthened and coordinated to ensure that all countries had the necessary "insurance" and no gaps remained, before the likely next economic crisis.

21. Other South–South mechanisms were providing important sources of long-term development finance, including the Asian Infrastructure Investment Bank. They contributed to promoting infrastructure at the regional level, financing industrialization and boosting productive capacity. Nonetheless, only a small part of finance was offered on concessional terms. Countries at different levels of development had critical needs that were not being met, and the South remained marginalized in the financial and economic system.

22. Some regions had found it difficult to set up South–South financial and monetary institutions that survived the test of time. Hence, consolidation of the global South was needed, with sufficient policy space so that institution building could mature within a framework of cooperation.

23. Some participants noted that, in order to enhance cooperation among developing countries, the principles for South–South cooperation should be upheld, flexibility and policy space should be provided to the global South and South–South cooperation should be driven by developing countries. Developing countries shared common interests. More than ever, it was important to promote solidarity in the global South if developing countries were not to be marginalized in the global trade and investment landscape.

Session II: South–South technology transfers and partnerships for technological innovation

24. Some speakers mentioned that intellectual property could be a tool that facilitated technology transfers.

25. Developing countries were increasingly commercializing technology. Trademarks and patents filed by developing countries for protection in other developing countries between 2004 and 2016 demonstrated the upward trend.

26. The disclosure of information and knowledge protected by intellectual property rights was important to ensure that the intellectual property system contributed to fostering innovation and creativity.

27. South–South cooperation in the area of intellectual property could be leveraged through initiatives promoted by United Nations agencies such as the World Intellectual Property Organization. The agency had created a series of platforms to promote exchange of technological information across developing countries. Platforms such as ones that enabled "matchmaking" among developing countries that developed technology and those that demanded such technology and capacity-building to learn how to find information on the matter and use it would be very useful.

28. The capacity to search and find technology-related information in spite of its availability in different languages was emphasized as an important issue.

29. United Nations agencies such as the World Intellectual Property Organization had several successful South–South stories in the field of intellectual property. They included, for example, platforms to exchange information about green technology and successful matchmaking between Indonesia and members of the African Regional Intellectual Property Organization.

30. Some speakers mentioned impediments to technology transfer for weaker economies. They included (a) information problems that deterred technology transactions; (b) market power associated with technology enforced by intellectual property; (c) unfavourable economic and governance conditions; and (d) inability of scientific and technical personnel to establish meaningful linkages with the global research community.

31. Successful experiences of technology transfer in developing countries showed that the primary focus should be on building local capacities. A set of pre-conditions was necessary for technology transfer related to infrastructure, macroeconomic stability, market size, access to finance and credit and availability of a skilled and trained labour force. The key message was that "technology never worked alone".

32. The capacity of a country to innovate relied largely on its knowledge base. The knowledge base of a society did not refer to education, but rather the structure and diversity of knowledge, including the production and export structure, technological knowledge embedded in the society and social belief systems that affected education choices. It was important for countries to have a good understanding of their knowledge base before adopting a new technology. Governments should be more proactive in creating enabling regulatory and institutional frameworks to foster innovation and structural changes. Social dialogues were important to build consensus on how to move forward with technology and innovation.

33. The main issues mentioned included the fact that many developing countries (mainly Asia) had become capital exporters and that those developing countries were actively negotiating investment treaties with other developing countries and new institutional collaboration schemes, such as public–private partnerships.

34. Some speakers also pointed out that technology should not be left to market forces alone. The future of work marked by disruptive technological change needed to be shaped by policies that supported learning and learning at an individual level, as well as learning within families, communities and networks. To remove barriers to technology transfer and absorption of technology, learning could not be only at an individual level; rather the unit of study had to be society and the knowledge base of society, as well as understanding regulations and institutions that were supporting learning.

35. There was a need to understand individual countries' production and trade structures, local exposure to technological advancements and legal and institutional frameworks.

36. The need for intellectual property provisions in trade treaties to provide flexibilities to enable less advanced economies to monetize intellectual property rights and benefit from the system, was highlighted.

37. The need for education and training to overcome silos, to enable absorbing technology and harnessing the potential of the digital economy, was also noted.

38. Looking forward, to promote technology transfer, a pragmatic approach was preferred especially considering the significant differences among developing countries. Indigenous resources and traditional knowledge should be valued and promoted through South–South cooperation.

Session III: South–South cooperation and "Industry 4.0"

39. "Industry 4.0" was providing new and unique opportunities for the South but, at the same time, also posing difficult challenges. The growing digital divide would widen in the absence of proactive policies to build digital infrastructure and digital capacities in developing countries.

40. Some speakers noted that the "fourth industrial revolution" had brought sweeping change to production, consumption, trade and investments. However, the disparity in terms of adoption, benefit and participation between developed and developing countries, as well as between developing countries, was significant.

41. Digital technologies brought opportunities and challenges for developing countries. The key challenges faced by most developing countries to benefiting from digital technologies included infrastructure, skills and service sector development.

42. Low adoption of digital technology was persistent in the South. There was a need for countries of the South to increase their capacity and competitiveness and to provide an enabling environment to develop and benefit from "Industry 4.0".

43. South–South cooperation could be part of the solution. It could involve exchanges of experiences and best practices on policies that enhanced the ecosystem for digital development and the wider "fourth industrial revolution". Cooperation could also focus on developing more concrete policies and schemes on financing for digital development.

44. Some participants stated that the UNCTAD 10-point progressive South–South digital cooperation agenda was an important contribution in the area and could be taken forward at the regional level, especially in Africa, providing support to small developing countries to help them advance digitally.

45. The South–South digital cooperation agenda needed to be supported by developing an innovation eco-system and corresponding skills ecosystem in developing countries. It was highly important to develop an innovation ecosystem, build a skills ecosystem and enhance understanding among the Southern community that the digital economy went beyond trade policymaking. Many issues such as the fiscal base, competition, data protection and regulatory frameworks were also important for the healthy development of the digital economy.

46. While recognizing the importance of digital technologies for shaping future economies, developing countries were also concerned about some issues related to the digital economy. Concerns included uneven development of electronic commerce (e-commerce), the possible disruptive effect of wider digital transformation on economic development and social cohesion, anti-competitive practices, weakening labour conditions and data security.

47. UNCTAD was called upon to conduct more analysis allowing developing countries to better understand the impact of "Industry 4.0" and digitalization and provide policy tools for developing countries to take advantage of "digital industrialization", including through deepening digital cooperation among the Southern community.

48. Some participants suggested that the debate on "Industry 4.0" needed more clarity as to what it should include. While e-commerce was clearly an important part of the debate, the scope of "Industry 4.0" – or the digital economy – was much broader, and a range of digital technologies was affecting industrialization and development. That broader scope needed to be considered by international organizations such as UNCTAD and the World Trade Organization.

49. Some participants said that developing countries needed to remain vigilant of developments at the World Trade Organization in relation to rules that advanced economies might want to negotiate on e-commerce and digital trade as such negotiations could have an impact on their policy space.

50. UNCTAD should conduct more analyses on South–South digital industrialization to help developing countries, especially African countries, to understand the complexities of digitalization and provide them with a way forward to catch up and narrow the digital gap.

C. Informal thematic consultation: Non-binding recommendations

UNCTAD presents, as a contribution to the BAPA+40 Conference, the following non-binding recommendations:

UNCTAD presents a set of non-binding recommendations as a contribution to the BAPA+40 Conference.

- South–South cooperation should be strengthened to help developing countries make the most of vibrant South–South trade, finance, investment and technology for sustainable development. Regional and country experiences need to be analysed to fully understand why the "rise of the South" has been uneven and release the catalytic potential of South–South growth.

- Innovations and deeper interactions in South–South financial and monetary cooperation should be seen as the foundations for providing pragmatic options that address Southern concerns, within the global system.

- South–South cooperation should be seen as a complement to, not a substitute for, North–South cooperation. Official development assistance commitments need to be met and deficiencies of the multilateral institutions addressed as well.

- South–South cooperation should support building productive capacity and structural transformation in the South, especially in Africa and LDCs. Strategic engagement with South–South value chains is needed to drive upgrading and diversification.

- Latin America, Asia and Africa need to strengthen partnerships across regions in order to spur trade and investment cooperation.

- The BAPA+40 Conference should provide broad-based support for revitalizing South–South trade cooperation at the interregional level, including through the Global System of Trade Preferences among Developing Countries.

- South–South technology transfers and partnerships should be promoted for technological innovation via, for example, platforms enabling "matchmaking" between developing countries that develop technology and those that demand such technology and mechanisms (such as the United Nations Commission on Science and Technology for Development) that facilitate sharing of successful experiences among Southern countries. UNCTAD and other relevant international organizations can provide the technical assistance developing countries could require to enable them to access technologies.

- Developing countries of the South should form the necessary partnerships to meet the challenges posed by Industry 4.0. South–South digital cooperation is also key to promoting digital industrialization in the South.

- Policies for promoting electronic commerce (e-commerce) should be complemented by appropriate digital industrial policymaking in Africa to ensure the region harnesses the broader benefits of digitalization.

- Developing countries, especially in Africa, and LDCs need to coordinate their position on future rules at the World Trade Organization in relation to e-commerce and digital trade, taking into account their policy space to engage in industrialization.

REFERENCES

References

Agosin MR, Larraín C and Grau N (2010). Industrial policy in Chile. Working Paper Series No. IDB-WP-170. Inter-American Development Bank.

Asian Infrastructure Investment Bank (2018). Asian Infrastructure Investment Bank Update. January 2018. Beijing.

Baldwin R (2011). Trade and industrialization after globalization's second unbundling: How building and joining a supply chain are different and why it matters. Working Paper No. 17716. National Bureau of Economic Research.

Barrowclough D and Gottshalk R (2018). Solidarity and the South: Supporting the new landscape of long-term development finance. Research Paper No. 24. UNCTAD.

Belt and Road Forum for International Cooperation (2017). Deliverables for the Belt and Road Forum for International Cooperation, May 2017.

Bloomberg (2015). One Belt, One Road: Assessing the economic impact of China's new Silk Road. Bloomberg Brief. 2 July.

Caixin (2017). Zhou Xiaochuan: "Belt and Road" investment finance should be market-oriented. March.

Chang HJ (2013). Industrial policy: Can Africa do it? In: Stiglitz JE, Lin JY and Patel E, eds. *The Industrial Policy Revolution II: Africa in the Twenty-first Century*. Palgrave Macmillan. New York:114–134.

Development Bank of Latin America (2018). New issue of CAF "Green Bonds" to foster sustainable development in Latin America. 16 August. Available at https://www.caf.com/en/currently/news/2018/08/new-issue-of-caf-green-bonds-to-foster-sustainable-development-in-latin-america/.

Dollar D (2018). Is China's development finance a challenge to the international order? *Asian Economic Policy Review*. 13(2):283–298.

Development Finance (2017). AIIB [Asian Infrastructure Investment Bank] set to lend US$2.5 billion in 2017. 24 January. Available at www.devfinance.net/aiib-set-lend-us2-5-billion-2017/ (accessed 31 October 2018).

Economic Commission for Latin America and the Caribbean (2014). *Strengthening Value Chains as an Industrial Policy Instrument: Methodology and Experience of ECLAC [Economic Commission for Latin America and the Caribbean] in Central America* (United Nations publication. Sales No. E.14.II.G.9. Santiago).

Economic Commission for Latin America and the Caribbean (2018). Digital Agenda for Latin America and the Caribbean. Sixth Ministerial Conference on the Information Society in Latin America and the Caribbean, Cartagena, Colombia. 18–20 April 2018.

European Commission (2018). The European Cloud Initiative. Available at https://ec.europa.eu/digital-single-market/en/%20european-cloud-initiative (accessed 31 October 2018).

Foster JB and McChesney RW (2011). The Internet's unholy marriage to capitalism. *Monthly Review*. 62(10):1–30.

Gereffi G (2014). Global value chains in a post-Washington Consensus world. *Review of International Political Economy*. 21(1):9–37.

Glenbrook and Southern African Development Community Banking Association (2017). Regional payments integration, financial inclusion and remittances in the Southern African Development Community (SADC): Reflections on a work in progress.

Good N (2017). Paving the way for a boom in trade growth. IHS Markit Editorial. 7 December.

Group of 77 and China (2018). Frontier Technologies Conference: Ensuring technology delivers for sustainable development. Concept note.

Hausmann R, Rodrik D and Sabel CF (2008). Reconfiguring industrial policy: A framework with an application to South Africa. Working Paper No. 168. Centre for International Development.

Hermann J (2010). Development banks in the financial-liberalization era: The case of BNDES [the National Economic and Social Development Bank] in Brazil. *CEPAL [Economic Commission for Latin America and the Caribbean] Review*. 100:189–204.

Institute of International Finance (2018). *Global Debt Monitor.* 9 July. Available at https://www.iif.com/publications/global-debt-monitor.

International Monetary Fund (2018). Macroeconomic developments and prospects in low-income developing countries: 2018. *Policy Report*. March.

International Telecommunication Union (2018). Buenos Aires Declaration: Artificial intelligence and the Internet of things in smart sustainable cities in Latin America. 30 May.

Kozul-Wright R and Poon D (2015). Development finance with Chinese characteristics? *Project Syndicate.* 20 May. Available at https://www.project-syndicate.org/commentary/china-silk-road-fund-development-financing-by-richard-kozul-wright-and-daniel-poon-2015-05?barrier=accesspaylog (accessed 31 October 2018).

Lin JY and Chang HJ (2009). Should industrial policy in developing countries conform to comparative advantage or defy it? A debate between Justin Lin and Ha-Joon Chang. *Development Policy Review*. 27(5):483–502.

Leahy J and Schipani A (2017). Brazil's development bank BNDES faces reform. *Financial Times*. 30 August.

Mack E and Faggian A (2013). Productivity and broadband: The human factor. *International Regional Science Review*. 36(3):392–423.

Mazzucato M (2013). The Entrepreneurial State: Debunking Public vs. Private Sector Myths. Anthem Press. London.

Middle East and North Africa Cloud Alliance (2017). Cloud Competitiveness Index 2017: Gulf Cooperation Council overview – Laying the foundation for digital transformation. Available at https://www.menacloud.org/Doc/MENACA%20 CCI%20(c).pdf (accessed 31 October 2018).

National Economic and Social Development Bank of Brazil (2017). Financial statements. 31 December.

Nayyar D (2015). Birth, life and death of development finance institutions in India. *Economic and Political Weekly*. 50(33):51–60.

Organization for Economic Cooperation and Development (2013). *Interconnected Economies: Benefiting from Global Value Chains – Synthesis Report.* Available at https://www.oecd.org/sti/ind/interconnected-economies-GVCs-synthesis.pdf.

Poon D (2018a). Asian Infrastructure Investment Bank: Experiments in scaling-up development finance. UNCTAD News. 27 March. Available at http://unctad.org/en/pages/newsdetails.aspx?OriginalVersionID=1704 (accessed 1 November 2018).

Poon D (2018b). China's overseas development finance: Policy tools and mechanisms. In: Jaguaribe A, ed. *Direction of Chinese Global Investments: Implications for Brazil.* Alexandre de Gusmão Foundation. Brasilia.

Reddy YV (2017). Development banking: Way forward. Presented at the 100th Annual Conference of the Indian Economic Association. Acharya Nagarjuna University. Guntur, Andhra Pradesh. National Stock Exchange of India – Indian Economic Association Lecture Series on Financial Economics. 29 December.

Rodrik D (2010). The return of industrial policy. *Project Syndicate.* 12 April. Available at https://www.project-syndicate.org/commentary/the-return-of-industrial-policy?barrier=accesspaylog.

Shanghai Stock Exchange and Association of Chartered Certified Accountants (2017). *The Belt and Road Initiative: Reshaping the Global Value Chain.* Association of Chartered Certified Accountants. London.

Stiglitz JE and Uy M (1996). Financial markets, public policy and the East Asian miracle. *World Bank Research Observer.* 11(2):249–276.

Studart R and Gallagher KP (2016). Infrastructure for sustainable development: The role of national development banks. Policy Brief 007. Global Economic Governance Initiative.

UNCTAD (2006). *The Least Developed Countries Report 2006: Developing Productive Capacities* (United Nations publication. Sales No. E.06.II.D.9. New York and Geneva).

UNCTAD (2012b). *Technology and Innovation Report 2012: Innovation, Technology and South–South Collaboration* (United Nations publication. Sales No. E.12.II.D.13. New York and Geneva).

UNCTAD (2013a). *World Investment Report 2013: Global Value Chains – Investment and Trade for Development* (United Nations publication. Sales No. E.13.II.D.5. New York and Geneva).

UNCTAD (2013b). *Economic Development in Africa Report 2013: Intra-African Trade – Unlocking Private Sector Dynamism* (United Nations publication. Sales No. E.13.II.D.2. Geneva).

UNCTAD, (2014a). *World Investment Report 2014: Investing in the Sustainable Development Goals – An Action Plan* (United Nations publication. Sales No. E.14.II.D.1. New York and Geneva).

UNCTAD (2014b). *The Oceans Economy: Opportunities and Challenges for Small Island Developing States* (United Nations publication. New York and Geneva).

UNCTAD (2015a). *Global Value Chains and South–South Trade* (United Nations publication. New York and Geneva).

UNCTAD (2015b). *World Investment Report 2015: Reforming International Investment Governance* (United Nations publication. Sales No. E.15.II.D.5. New York and Geneva).

UNCTAD (2015c). *Investment Policy Framework for Sustainable Development.* UNCTAD/DIAE/PCB/2015/5. Geneva.

UNCTAD (2016a). *Trade and Development Report, 2016: Structural Transformation for Inclusive and Sustained Growth* (United Nations publication. Sales No.E.16.II.D.5. New York and Geneva).

UNCTAD (2016b). *Economic Development in Africa Report 2016: Debt Dynamics and Development Finance in Africa* (United Nations publication. Sales No. E.16.II.D.3. New York and Geneva).

UNCTAD (2016c). *The Least Developed Countries Report 2016: The Path to Graduation and Beyond: Making the Most of the Process* (United Nations publication. Sales No. E.16.II.D.9. New York and Geneva).

UNCTAD (2016d). *Review of Maritime Transport 2016.* (United Nations publication. Sales No. E.16.II.D.7. New York and Geneva).

UNCTAD (2016e). Nairobi Maafikiano. TD/519/Add.2. Nairobi. 5 September.

UNCTAD (2016f). Data Protection Regulations and International Data Flows: Implications for Trade and Development (United Nations publication. New York and Geneva).

UNCTAD (2017a). *Trade and Development Report 2017: Beyond Austerity – Towards a Global New Deal* (United Nations publication. Sales No. E.17.II.D.5. New York and Geneva).

UNCTAD (2017b). *The Least Developed Countries Report 2017: Transformational Energy Access* (United Nations publication. Sales No. E.17.II.D.6. New York and Geneva).

UNCTAD (2017c). *The Role of Development Banks in Promoting Growth and Sustainable Development in the South* (United Nations publication. New York and Geneva).

UNCTAD (2017d). *World Investment Report 2017: Investment and the Digital Economy* (United Nations publication. Sales No. E.17.II.D.3. Geneva).

UNCTAD (2017e). *Fishery Exports and the Economic Development of Least Developed Countries: Bangladesh, Cambodia, the Comoros, Mozambique and Uganda* (United Nations publication. New York and Geneva).

UNCTAD (2017f). *Information Economy Report 2017: Digitalization, Trade and Development* (United Nations publication. Sales No. E.17.II.D.8. New York and Geneva).

UNCTAD (2017g). *The "New" Digital Economy and Development.* UNCTAD Technical Notes on ICT for Development No. 8 (United Nations publication. Geneva).

UNCTAD (2017h). How can science and technology deliver on development? UNCTAD brings together the experts in Geneva to find out. Information Note. UNCTAD/PRESS/IN/2017/002. 25 January. Available at https://unctad.org/en/Pages/InformationNoteDetails.aspx?OriginalVersionID=79 (accessed 1 November 2018).

UNCTAD (2017i). ASYCUDA – Automated System for Customs Data: Streamlining customs management. In: *UNCTAD Toolbox: Delivering Results,* revised (United Nations publication. Geneva).

UNCTAD (2017j). Celebrating 15 years of cooperation between customs of the Pacific Region and UNCTAD. ASYCUDA Newsletter: UNCTAD Division on Technology and Logistics (Geneva).

UNCTAD (2018a). *Trade and Development Report 2018: Power, Platforms and the Free Trade Delusion* (United Nations publication. Sales No. E.18.II.D.7. New York and Geneva).

UNCTAD (2018b). *World Investment Report 2018: Investment and New Industrial Policies* (United Nations publication. Sales No. E.18.II.D.4. New York and Geneva).

UNCTAD (2018c). *Scaling up Finance for the Sustainable Development Goals: Experimenting with Models of Multilateral Development Banking* (United Nations publication. New York and Geneva).

UNCTAD (2018d). Fostering development gains from e-commerce and digital platforms. TD/B/EDE/2/2. 14 February.

UNCTAD (2018e). *South–South Digital Cooperation: A Regional Integration Agenda.* (United Nations publication. New York and Geneva).

UNCTAD (2018f). Digital economy data gap risks widening inequalities, UNCTAD says. UNCTAD News. 23 March.

UNCTAD (2018g). Working Group on Measuring E-commerce and the Digital Economy. TD/B/EDE/2/3. 21 February.

UNCTAD (2018h). Solomon Islands customs agency collects record $1 billion. UNCTAD News. 1 March. Available at https://unctad.org/en/pages/newsdetails. aspx?OriginalVersionID=1674 (accessed 1 November 2018).

UNCTAD (forthcoming). Regional integration and Southern Africa: A platform for electricity sustainability.

UNCTAD and Food and Agriculture Organization of the United Nations (2017). *Commodities and Development Report 2017: Commodity Markets, Economic Growth and Development* (United Nations publication. New York and Geneva).

United Nations, Economic and Social Council (2012). Innovation, research, technology transfer for mutual advantage, entrepreneurship and collaborative development in the information society. E/CN.16/2012/2. 12 March.

United Nations, Economic and Social Council (2018). Building digital competencies to benefit from existing and emerging technologies, with a special focus on gender and youth dimensions. E/CN.16/2018/3. 1 March.

United Nations Development Programme (2013). *Human Development Report 2013: The Rise of the South: Human Progress in a Diverse World*. New York.

Van Alstyne MW, Parker GG and Choudary SP (2016). Pipelines, platforms, and the new rules of strategy. *Harvard Business Review*. 94(4): 54–60.

Wade RH (2003). What strategies are viable for developing countries today? The World Trade Organization and the shrinking of "development space". *Review of International Political Economy.* 10(4):621–644.

Waters J (2017). "Unimpeded trade" in Central Asia: A trade facilitation challenge. Transnational Dispute Management. Available at www.transnational-dispute-management.com (accessed 1 November 2018).

Wang W (2015). Implications of the Belt and Road Initiative to sustainable development of global transport and supply. Presented at the Multi-year Expert Meeting on Transport, Trade Logistics and Trade Facilitation (UNCTAD), fourth session. Geneva. 14–16 October 2015.

World Trade Organization, Fung Global Institute and Nanyang Technological University (2013). *Global Value Chains in a Changing World.* World Trade Organization. Geneva.

Xi JP (2017). Speech delivered at the opening ceremony of the Belt and Road Forum for International Cooperation. 14 May. Available at www.xinhuanet.com/english/2017-05/14/c_136282982.htm (accessed 1 November 2018).

Xu QY (2016). CDB [China Development Bank]: Born bankrupt, born shaper. Presented at the meeting on the future of national development banks held by the Brazilian Development Bank, the Development Bank of Latin America and the Initiative for Policy Dialogue. Rio de Janeiro. 15 and 16 September.

Zhu Y (2015). Chinese steel capacity may go west with One Belt One Road. Bloomberg Professional Service. 23 June.